Crowned Butterfly

Saved, Submitted and Subjected

Crowned Butterfly

Saved, Submitted and Subjected

Skyye Howze

ISBN: 9781690626183

The scriptures in this book are quoted from:
- King James Version in Public Domain
- New International Version (NIV) Holy Bible, New International Version®, NIV® Copyright ©1973, 1978, 1984, 2011 by Biblica, Inc.® Used by permission. All rights reserved worldwide

For information on the content of this book, email
skyyehowze@yahoo.com

WrightStuf Consulting, LLC
www.wrightstuf.com
info@wrightstuf.com

Printed in the United States of America

Contents

Introduction

Prelude

As I walk into my transparency, it didn't mean I didn't struggle with anything, it didn't mean I didn't fall short, it most definitely didn't mean I didn't make any mistakes. The more I walked with God the more the devil attacked me. In fact, things started to shift, going left.

During this particular season, I will share more about how I became a "CROWNED BUTTERFLY," and in the midst of this season, how I also found myself seeking God when I wanted to, going back into my old ways, doing things how I used to do them, and just dismissing God totally. This journey was never over. Not only did I overcome, but God spared me and pulled me through while my wings were stretched, and I was forced to fly. ☺

The time will come when you think the devil has retired from messing with you. Not so. Anything he can do to distract your walk with God, he will do it. Like the bible says, the devil is only out *to kill, steal, and destroy, seeking whom he may devour*. He almost took me out until God put his fence around my life. I tell you, I haven't been the same since God anchored me. As I pour into you about how Jesus freed me, I will spill about how I was robbed out of my freedom that I so desperately longed for, but gained it back tripled.

I pray that my testimony help you get to God quickly and live according to his will and not yours. The joy of being saved is all I care to be. No matter what I went through, I fought to live this life and become the woman I was destined to be. I hope you find that fight too, so you can wear your "Crown" victoriously with much happiness, allowing yourself to walk full force in your DESTINY just as I have!!

Chapter One

Broken Engagement

In my first book, "A Broken That's Unspoken," I talked about my (now ex-) fiancé. Things inevitably turned out for the worst. I knew moving him in could either hinder me or help me. No, we were not married when he came to live in my home and yes, God was definitely not pleased.

February 16, 2016, Devon proposed to me in the middle of my living room floor. He placed the ring on the wrong hand. I'm not sure if he was nervous or just didn't know any better, but eventually, he switched and placed it on the third finger, left hand. I was excited and I said YES!! We kissed following up with a hug, but I felt no peace in my heart about it. In fact, I wasn't happy; I felt uneasy the whole entire time. I ignored the feeling of conviction because this was something I wanted so badly. One of my biggest heart's desires was to be married. I figured if I go through with it, he could possibly be the husband I wanted and a father for my kids. I mean, I put up with everything that came with him so I figured what else could go wrong. From that

1

day forward, everything was falling in place. At least, I thought they were. We went on about our day celebrating; went out to eat and had a lovely time. The whole time we were out, I could hear God speaking to me, telling me not to go through with this engagement because disappointment was going to take place. I wasn't trying to hear what God had to say.

I was doing my own thing because I wanted this man. But my heart didn't need him. After all the shacking, living together and now soon-to-become his wife, could this be my big break of trying to do the right thing? Well, he didn't have a job so guess who was taking care of everything? Me. I believed things would get better. I always believed in giving a person the benefit of the doubt; giving them the space to get themselves together, but with him, I felt used and taken for granted. For some odd reason, the fact that we dated an entire year before he proposed, I thought maybe he would step it up and bring something to the table financially. But I must give him credit; while I worked, he made sure food was cooked, the house was sparkling clean, and he watched my kids when needed. When I couldn't afford daycare, my daughter went with her other (dad's) family. Devon looked after my son, but I was still always skeptical about it because my son was still going through his premature stage and "Mommy" was the only one who knew what to do. Of course, I instructed Devon on what to do in case of an emergency. Besides, he was the only help I had. Despite anything we faced, he was there for me somewhat in his own way and I was thankful for that.

I loved the help that I was getting around the house, but the bills began to pile up and he still didn't have a job. I explained to him that if he didn't have a job, then he would have to leave. He was furious. We had a big argument and he stormed out of the house, slamming the door behind him. He was filled with anger and mad about having to find a job so then I understood he was using me. Because of his actions, the doubt of wondering eventually kicked in. I prayed because I needed God and money. Even though I wasn't doing right, I know God was still going to provide. I'm a faithful tither that makes big sacrifices and I always believed that when I take care of God's house, I shall never lack for long.

God won't keep sparing me in my mess, so I'm texting and calling Devon. No answer. It's getting late. I wasn't sure if he had his key or not. The minute I laid down the doorbell rings. It's HIM!! He gave me some lame excuse as to why he wasn't answering. On top of that, he smelled like he had been smoking. He lied. I smelled it on his breath before his clothing. I didn't say anything; I just went to bed.

When I thought things were getting better, it all turned out badly. I woke up to a phone call from my temporary job telling me they didn't need me anymore.

Since I went through the whole hiring process, I figured it was permanent. So now we were both without jobs. I needed a miracle. Bills were due that following week. All I could ponder is where would I get this money from. *Lord I need your help IMMEDIATELY!!* I explained to Devon how he needed to get a job; it was time to search. He agreed so we prayed about it, filled out applications in lots of places.

I needed a few items from Walmart, so we went. As we entered the store, the Lord spoke to me telling me to tell Devon to ask if they were hiring. We ended up stopping an employee who just so happened to be the district manager of Walmart. He told Devon that they did need someone and to go online to fill out an application. He had already applied online, so the manager asked him to come back the following day and ask for the district manager.

We headed home and got things done around the house. Devon started dinner while I attended to the kids. He decided to take the trash out and left his phone on the kitchen counter. Normally, I wouldn't go through his phone, but this time I couldn't resist what I was feeling deep inside. It was time for him to be exposed. I always believed that what goes on in the dark shall soon come to the light. This was the day for me to find out everything.

I check his phone and I see that he's pouring his heart out to his child's mother. I was crushed. My heart sank. Everything he was telling her, he was telling me, too. I said silently, "This dirty bastard." It was clear that he still had deep feelings for her that never went away and he wanted to be with her. I was pained with total silence. He came back in the house to finish cooking the food. I didn't say one word. I didn't allow my feelings to dictate my actions. I went on like I knew nothing.

We ate dinner while watching a movie; just spending time. My thoughts begin to run deeper than a river flowing with ongoing water that never reaches its destination. I have no job, bills are still due, now I find out that Devon's heart is not only for me but for someone else, as well. I didn't know what I was going to do. Life seemed unbearable. I felt like I couldn't make it, but I knew God was going to make a way sooner or later. I had to really depend on him and trust him in the midst of this raging storm. I began to shake myself out of my feelings. Even though I knew how he felt for her, I still insisted on giving him my body to feel secure in my insecurities because sex gave me a high that made me feel alive, even when I was dying inside.

Afterward, Devon fell asleep. I left the room and went into prayer. I needed God's help and we both needed jobs. I prayed for about two hours. God began to show me things in a spiritual realm dealing with my book. Not my ideas but God's ideas for my first book that I had down inside me, yet prolonging the process of writing. I wasn't sure how I would pull it off because I knew nothing about writing a book. Once God was done dealing with me, I got the kids ready for bed. As I tucked them in softly following up with prayer over their little lives, I sat in the room until they both fell asleep. The next morning came and life began to really sink in. Things were going badly. I needed a breakthrough. Heck!! I needed a miracle.

Before dropping the kids off for daycare, I prayed to God on the thin faith I was operating in, carrying it slothful, begging and pleading for him to give me a job because, at this point, I was desperately in need of finances. I wasn't sure how I would make it, but I had no other choice but to trust God. I went on with my day; going into deep thought. I got so deep in my thoughts, God came in the midst and spoke to me; telling me to ask the owner of the daycare where my kids attended if she needed any help. I didn't ponder on it I said okay, God; I simply obeyed. As soon as God stopped speaking to me, Devon started 'something' - an argument - with me. I knew it was the enemy, plus I felt he was only doing it as an excuse to leave. He had his stuff packed up already. All I could do was crumble in my spirit. My heart went numb as it almost stopped beating. It was that intense. I began to weep, and I mean uncontrollable weeping. It just didn't make sense. I had no understanding at all. I was being broken from someone I thought loved me and was happy for me and when he left, it was my most trying time. That really showed me that he was never it in for me. He was only in it to benefit his needs. So how am I supposed to react to that, knowing that this man proposed to me as if he wanted to spend the rest of his life with me? I mean, what was his motive to begin with?

The clock was ticking. It was close to time to pick up the kids. I had to pull myself together because I had to be prepared for what God had assigned to me. My car acted as if it didn't want to start! All I'm thinking now is *LOOK at this devil, what else could go wrong?* With a deep sigh, I recognized that everything was hitting me hard all at once. The car finally started after trying to turn the ignition multiple times. I drove to get the kids, and as I held a conversation with the owner of the daycare, I was led to ask what was spoken to me when I was in deep thought at home. Mrs. McHover, "Are you hiring? Or need any help?" I asked boldly.

She replied, "Yes, as a matter of fact, I am looking for a secretary to run the front desk for me. Are you available?"

I quickly said, "Yes Ma'am! When would you like for me to start?"

"Next week will be fine. You could start on Wednesday."

It was just amazing how God opened up a door SUDDENLY. That really took me by surprise, and although I was happy about the move of God, I still had one problem - Devon not having a job. That was a very big burden on me because financially, we both needed income to take care of the kids and living expenses. But I still had hope and I knew God wasn't going to let me down. He showed me that no matter what takes place, he will always see me through.

I started to think of his goodness. I was getting excited. Tears of joy began to form because not only was I blessed with a job, I was close to graduating with my associate degree. Now here's the set up with God. To work at a daycare, you have to have a degree, a background check, and a list of other requirements. BUT GOD showed me favor before my degree reached my hands. God did a mighty shift. Now that was a supernatural miracle only God could do, after seeing that my faith increased, and my trust expanded.

I went home to share the good news with my fiancé. He didn't seem so happy for me. With all the financial problems we were facing, you would think he would be ecstatic for me. Nope! He seemed as if he was jealous. As my spirit started to feel vexed, I switched the conversation asking, "Babe, do you want to go to bible study with me tonight?"

He insisted that he would stay home. The impression he put on around me vs. the one he portrayed to others made me see his true colors. He was getting a little too relaxed with the Word, especially when it came down to church!!! He wasn't doing what a man of God was supposed to be doing. It seemed as though he used God to get what he needed and where he wanted to be.

My discernment kicked in fast. I didn't argue about his refusal to go to bible study. I just said, "I will pray for you," as I headed out the door with the kids. I wasn't going to let anyone stop me from going to church. Even if I didn't have peace at home, I would find it at church, so being in God's presence was all I longed for. I could always take my pain and leave it at the altar, and gain strength to deal with what was left in the midst of the situations I faced daily. After all, I needed a breakthrough in my home, so I got up for prayer.

I was going through so much; I just couldn't fathom what would happen next. *God, why am I facing such hard times?* God spoke to me telling me not to hold on to Devon. *Get rid of him.* If I didn't, there would be more destruction. If I chose to disobey. I said okay, God. You know what's best.

When we returned to the house, Devon was nowhere to be found. At least I could say the house was clean, food was on the stove, and the kids' clothes were ready for school and bath time. I was so appreciative for that. I thanked him for trying. It was a breather for me. He always eased my load, but there were so many other burdens that were weighing me down, and financially I still wasn't secure.

Now, normally I would go looking for him or blowing his phone up until I felt like it was about to blow apart, but not this time. This time I was humble. Instead of the usual insecurities, I started brainstorming for my book. Adding to the ideas Devon helped come up with, as well, for the book. Gathering my thoughts, getting things in alignment on paper, praying and reading the bible until drifting off to sleep. I began to dream:

The wind is blowing forcefully, knocking everything over, causing mass destruction to people, places, and things. Damage is upon everything and everybody. It is traumatizing. Everyone is forced to move out of its path. The clouds get darker and darker. People are screaming. No one can see anything. A big blaze of fire comes from out of nowhere. The screaming is so intense. I speak in my heavenly language for comfort. The more I speak, the more the fire backs off of me....

I jumped, pouring in sweat as I heard the doorbell rang repeatedly. I just remained there in total shock of the glimpse of the dream that I had. I tried to write it down but couldn't because the doorbell rang again. I'm like dang it, I just couldn't grasp what was taking place in all that God was showing me but eventually the revelation would come sooner or later. I tried to get myself together. I was just in awe. I had slept so long not realizing it was the next morning. The doorbell rang again. As I looked through the peephole of my door, I took a deep breath. Two social service workers from the Department of Human Services - DHS – were at my door. I was a tad bit confused, but I opened the door with a smile. I invited the two women to come in to have a seat. They introduced themselves and told me why they were visiting. My heart started beating extremely fast because I didn't know what to expect. I asked, "Is there a problem?"

One of the women replied, "We are a little concerned about the calls we received. The reason we are here this morning is because we got multiple calls about the wellbeing of your children."

Tears formed in my eyes and all I could think about was if my kids were taken away from me, I would literally die. They looked around the house. Everything was clean, my kids were clean, food was in the kitchen, etc. One said, "Everything looks good, Miss Howze. You got your stuff together. Why would someone call us on you?"

I stood there in total shock. Then she asked me, "What is it that you do?"

I couldn't have been prouder to brag on God. God knew DHS was coming; I didn't. I said, "Well God has blessed me with a job doing secretary work at a daycare and also I will be graduating getting my AA degree in May." They smiled and I added, "Before going back to complete what I started, I was also a student at Delta State University; a senior with four classes away from getting my BS degree in Social Work."

They were amazed and encouraged me to finish. Not only that, they offered me a job in my field, once I finished Delta State (but I never finished there).

I was set up for a blessing but someone else was after me trying to destroy my life through my kids. The weapon formed but it didn't prosper. If someone tries to set you up for a blessing, let them, because God will make an impossible move to see that blessing through. He did it for me because I was walking in obedience, being faithful, and sacrificing even when I was hurting to the core.

I had to be at work at 12 noon. Still, no Devon. So, once the social workers left, I got all of us ready and we were headed out the door, when, I got a call saying Devon was in jail. I'm like, "Oh Lord, what is really going on? Geesh."

He had a warrant for his arrest from something he did in his past. I'm already uptight about the situation at hand with DHS. Now this. I need God like never before because I'm being tried and clearly about to lose my mind. I hung up the phone.

Pulling up to work, my mind was all over the place. I said a quick prayer (and yes God hears those too) before getting out the car to build myself up because to be honest, I didn't know what I had to face at work. I got the kids out of the car, got them to their classrooms before I started working. Mrs. McHover was there. She gave me a run-down of what I'd be doing. I got focused and got to my assignments.

My phone kept vibrating. An unfamiliar number kept calling so I went to the restroom to answer it. Devon was calling from jail. He said he had a warrant for child support. As I was getting ready to tell him I had started my new job, another call came in and interrupted our conversation. It was my advisor from college reminding me about my graduation fee, graduation practice, and to make sure I had all of my required credits to graduate. Devon hung up. I couldn't call back because I was at work on a new job; and well, because he was in jail. I just continued to work.

Work was okay. *Once I adjust to the environment and people, I'll open up, but until then I'm staying to myself.* As the thoughts faded away, I started feeling the tension of being stressed from life. I sat at my desk filing paperwork. I opened my bible and God took me to Psalms 62:5. "My soul wait thou only upon God; for my expectations is from him." I read it over and over until it resonated in my spirit. God began to speak:

Daughter, this is the season of growth. There will be trying times that will try to knock you down. Things and people will come along and cause a deep hurt but it's going to help you push forward in your calling. Please trust me in the process. I will be there to catch you when you fall.

Tears fell down my face. I was refreshed from the revelation God had given to my situation. I was just so concerned I couldn't stand what I was facing but I had to go through it.

FINALLY, my shift was over. I drove to the house. I made it. Devon was standing at the door asking for my help. I said, "What is it now with an attitude, and when did you get out of jail?"

He said, "My mother bonded me out. I told her to call you to let you know." He told me that he needed money for his P.O. because he was behind. I insisted that I would help when I was able to but there was nothing I could do at the time. He gave me this sob story that I wasn't listening to. He tried to come into the house. He did the best he could to try to get me to fall for what he was saying. I said No and slammed my door in his face. I was in a place in my life where I needed God so badly, I was not about to allow any drama or distractions to take my focus. This time I took heed. Devon got mad and cursed me out. I didn't say one word. I smiled, pondering on should I go to sleep or write. The phone rang. It was the pretty lady CJ asking me if the wedding was still on. I just didn't have the energy to talk about that. I was tired from all that I went through in that one day. I ended the conversation with *I love you, I'm about to get dinner started and clean the house. I will get back with you later!* I hung up the phone, finished with everything around the house, and I was so exhausted. As I lay down to relax, I found myself drifting off into a deep sleep. I begin to dream:

I was outside my grandmother's house. A big dark cloud covered only her house. I'm walking up going into the door, the lights are off. I reach to pull the switch up and I see my family held hostage by strange-looking men. They had some stuff that they had in their hands that looked like grease and whatever the substance was you could rub it on anyone, and it will knock them out instantly. As they tried to put the substance on me, they couldn't knock me out with it, so the man screamed loudly SHOOT HER, SHE MUST DIE!! I laughed and said I'm covered in the blood and I prayed to the heavens fell down. When I did so, the men faded away turning into dust one by one. The dark cloud left from over the house and my family was rising up together loving on one another.

My phone vibrated. Still half asleep, I read the text message from the pretty lady CJ. She found me a dress and we would go shopping for my veil and other things that we needed for the wedding. I was excited but had mix emotions too because I didn't know how to tell her the wedding was off. I was so nervous, but I accepted the date, stopped texting and God began to take me into a deep worship. I followed with a prayer and the word because now these dreams were getting ridiculous and I don't understand what God is showing me. Whew! This was too much to handle. My God, this is a lot to take on. I'm still premature in the spiritual realm. I was clueless as to what God was doing with me in my dreams. This stuff was SCARY!!

I started getting myself and the kids ready to head out the door. We were leaving the house every morning at 7 a.m. My life revolved around my job and my kids. This was something I had to get used to. It was pretty rough and draining, but I had to pay bills and take care of my children. No matter how challenging life got, I had to work hard because I just didn't have the proper help that I needed. I prayed for some extra hours, hoping I could go from part-time to full-time. I got to work, got finished with what I had left from the other day so I could stay ahead, and even if I had to, help others. I toured the daycare center. I started to see that things were unorganized so, being the very neat and clean person that I am, I cleaned every room in the center. I started in the back and vowed to work on one room at a time until I was able to get all the rooms done. I was told I wouldn't do all that extra work because I wasn't getting paid for it, but it wasn't about the money; it was about having a clean spirit. I couldn't work in cluttered environments. My spirit would be vexed. I'm very organized and I did it from the kindness of my heart, not for recognition. To be comfortable and to feel free in my spirit.

When I got a break, instead of eating, I would go to the park or either home to finish writing on my book(s). I was so determined to get my assignment done for God. I was working and writing on those two books because I knew one day my story would be the voice for many. So, I was led to go to the park to not only write but listen to God. In the midst of writing, I had a nervous breakdown. I cried out to God like I had never done before. As I'm giving God all that I had, I begin to feel the pressure lift up off my body. God exposed the fear I was facing as being a single mother full time, being an employee, and writing full time on both books.

God, I need you now, I screamed over and over. As the tears fell on the paper, I felt a cool breeze go all over my body and I looked up, the trees were whistling at me. God ministered to me through the trees and from the leaves. God said: **You have been leaning on that one leaf (Troubles) for so long, it's time to get out your comfort zone. Step out on faith; hold tight to the tree (God) so you can be free, healed and sane. No more attacks. While this one leaf causes more damage than you could handle, you are about to see the whole truth that's there to repair, restore, redeem, relieve, revive and remove so you could be a better you.**

A sense of peace came over me. I smiled and couldn't stop thanking God as I headed back to work. I walked in the office seeing Mrs. McHover was sitting at her desk. She was doing paperwork and telling me how she liked my work ethic and how I worked hard. She insisted that I should be a businessperson because I worked like one. She began to encourage me to go further in school. As the conversation carried on, she enlightened me to go to some classes to become the assistant director. I told her I wasn't ready for that just yet. We both laughed, and then she said well when you are ready. Let me know. I was in awe because I knew God was truly up to something, I just couldn't put my hand on it. I finished my work for the day. It was the weekend. Hooray! I could get some sleep, LOL.

I received a phone call. It was Devon crying and pouring his heart out to me and I listened. I let him cry and express his feelings, but I didn't fall for it anymore. Normally, I would hang up in his face, but I listened and as he ended, I said, "God bless your soul," with a soft and kind voice, then politely getting off the phone. I got home and relaxed; had the kids in the bed with me. They enjoyed our time together at home because I couldn't be mommy at work. It was different. So, I read the kids bible to them, playing worship music to keep the atmosphere flowing in the home. Even though I needed a break from them, I knew I needed them ever the most in my presence. It's like they could sense when my heart was aching. They would soothe me with much affection. Unknowingly, we all drifted off to sleep to the soothing music.

I woke up Saturday morning. I must have been exhausted. I'd never slept through to the next morning. I wake up throughout the night. I felt so refreshed. I started the day off with a worship in my spirit singing, "Thank you, Lord for being so good to me." I left the room humming the rest of the song to start my Saturday breakfast. Ordinarily, I would use this day to clean, but I had my shopping date for veils and dress fittings with the pretty lady CJ. After cooking and feeding the kids and myself, I got us all ready to go to Greenville, MS to the bridal store. This was exciting and bittersweet all at once. I wanted desperately to be married. Something my heart craved for but I'm living with this broken engagement. Everything turned out for the worse. There was no turning back because God removed Devon after he saw how he was hindering my walk for Christ.

CJ knocked on the door. As always, I welcomed her with opened arms and with a big smile. It was always a joy to see her. Just to be in her presence alone made life comfortable. My kids were just as crazy about her as I was. It was easy to pour out to her. I could trust her with everything. She knew all of my business. I was okay with that. I knew it would never travel, so as I vented to her about the issues of life, I never brought up the broken engagement. I didn't want to turn her smile into a frown.

We were having an awesome day. We finally made it to the store to try on the veils. I tried on the first veil and it was so breathtaking. I looked in the mirror and tears formed as I stared at myself, seeing how beautiful I would have been as a bride. Then God spoke, saying, *As you can see through the veil of decoration, things may be pretty on the outside, but somethings will be ugly once the veil is pulled up.* He continued on to say, *Life is about to turn for you, things are about to unfold right before your eyes.*

I started to feel uneasy in my spirit, and as my heart was racing, I snatched the veil off. CJ asked, "Are you okay? You look worried."

I said, "Everything is fine, just nervous." We left the store and we went to her cousin's house to do the fitting for my dress. The dress was so beautiful. I tried it on, and it was fitted all the way up to my back. The zipper stuck and I knew then it was a sign that no matter how beautiful the scene looked, the story was not to be completed. I was falling apart on the inside. As we got on the road, I stared out the window; I thought, *just as long as these streets are, so is my journey. Will I ever get to my destiny?* I pondered and my thoughts changed.

I had church the next day and I started to think about what I would teach the kids for Sunday school. My thoughts flowed deep as I tried to understand what God was saying to me. My thinking pattern roamed; I couldn't stay in one area, then the phone rang and distracted my thoughts all together. Devon was calling. I didn't answer because it was either two things he wanted: (1) He would try to give me a sob story to move back in or (2) He needed me to help him with something. Since I didn't answer his call, he sent a text. I wasn't picking up at this point in my life. I couldn't afford to lose focus. I had to keep my mind sound.

When we arrived home, I thanked CJ and told her I loved her with a goodnight kiss on her cheek. Being that I couldn't sleep, I sacrificed staying up to get a lesson together for Sunday school. I was so excited; I was bubbly in my spirit. God was downloading so much stuff in me; he had a special word for them that I couldn't wait to share. After finishing up, I was getting ready to go into prayer when Devon called again. I'm like, *Oh Lord, I wish he would just go away,* and I let the phone ring. I pushed through for prayer because honestly, I didn't feel like it, but I prayed anyhow. I found myself so deep in praying I fell asleep. I dreamed: *I was walking down the sidewalk going into a store. Devon ended up coming in the store wearing a red tuxedo (represented Satan) and Jabari had on a white tuxedo (represented Angel). They were standing beside one another. I didn't want him to see me in the store, so I hid behind the curtain and I told him to hold on while I was getting help with somethings.*

Once I was finished, Devon was gone leaving Jabari standing in the middle of the floor. I screamed: DEVON WHERE ARE YOU, I got no answer. I started to panic. I rushed out of the store trying to get in the car, fumbling with my keys. As I'm doing so, a guy came up behind me and snatched Jabari and me up from behind. He put us in an all-black truck with no windows. I screamed as loud as I could so someone could hear me. The man put a gun to Jabari's head and told me to shut up before he killed my son.

I still didn't shut up. I started screaming JESUS! JESUS! JESUS! He backed, up calling Devon on the phone saying, "I got your fiancée. What do you want me to do with this woman? He insists that I get on the phone. I started crying telling him that I needed him, I'm not safe, and please come get us. He said he will see us soon and hung up the phone. I'm confused and so scared. We pull up to an abandoned house that looked like a jail. The man threw us off the truck; taking us in this creepy place, basically leaving us to die. I saw Devon walking in. I smiled so hard, but as I saw this woman come from behind him, the smile faded. I'm mumbling under my breath saying, what the hell is this? Right there in my face he began to have sex with this woman. After they finished, he told me, "I will not rescue you I'm leaving you here to die. I'm with who I want to be with."

I woke up in a cold sweat. Tears rolled down my face and my heart was sinking in this hour. God took me back to the veil fitting. My dream was a revelation and now it was up to me to take heed. At the same time, be watchful and very alert in the spirit. I was so furious about this dream.

I had church service in a few hours. I was broken but still had to minister in the midst of my pain. *God, why me?* I asked as I fell to my knees. *This isn't fair. I needed you to take this pain away. I couldn't make it without you.* I had to talk to God because the dream messed me up. I was a total wreck and I couldn't see my way. I knew he was preparing me for something; I just didn't understand at that very moment but in due time I'll be equipped to wear my crown.

Chapter Two

Sacrifices

I'm now in a place of suffering. I got myself together quickly, heading out the door, going to church. I'm driving down the highway; mind all over the place. Tears are still falling. We made it to the church. Pulling into the parking lot, I'm still in awe of the revelation and dream. I just couldn't get myself focused. I began to feel sick. Suddenly, it had gotten so bad; I had to pep talk myself to get out the car. I washed the tears away as fast as I could. I started to see cars pulling into the parking lot, so I put on this fake smile while I was dying internally. If only they knew what I was feeling. I just couldn't shake that excruciating pain that took over my whole entire body; weighing me down like a ton of bricks.

However, I always believed in being on time. Prompt, to be exact, so I could get my lesson prepared for my Sunday school class. To my surprise, no kids showed up. I waited. Time was consistently moving, still no kids. I was so hot and furious, and I was literally about to snap right there in church because this had happened to me over and over again. Due to the lack of participation by the other church children, I ended up teaching only my kids every time. It was not fair. I had stayed up all night preparing a word for God's little angels who didn't show up. But at the end of the day, I counted it all joy because I was pouring into my own children. Whether they understood or not, they would have Jesus deeply incased in their little souls.

Sunday school was finally over and we were flowing into the regular service. I just sat there. It was so dead in this church. Everything was so traditional and religious; the program never changed. It seemed as though nothing or nobody was led by the spirit to do things differently. The service was always prompted to go as outlined or whatever the pastor said. That was very sickening to my spirit. This dry place was already tormenting my soul. I got so much going on in my life, I didn't feel God, so I debated in my mind, *should I stand to force worship out of* me or should I just sit?

I no longer knew why I still attended this church. I joined the church when I was 20 years old, backslid for two years, came back three years later to rededicate my life like God told me to, and then for two more years which all added of to seven years total. (Completion) I sensed my time was almost up of being a part of that ministry.

I had grown tired of the same stuff. It was too familiar. I knew what would take place before it happened because it was constant and routine. Sad to say, when the word was brought forward, I was not excited. In fact, my spirit was vexed. I was drained, and the way it was preached was never understandable to me, so not only did I feel confused, I needed clarity on a fresh word.

Since my spirit had outgrown that ministry, I said, "God, I just want to get out of this. I'm hurting, I'm frustrated, I'm tired, and I'm at the end of my rope"

God said: "Don't move until I say move. I'm birthing something in you that requires you to grow under construction."

I had to embrace that. I didn't have it all together in my molding for Christ. I allowed myself to make noise to construct a new life. The plan was designed in my head. I was so desperate to put everything together myself with the necessary tools to use for my life, but it wasn't the appointed time. I was still under God's construction. He was still building. My patience had run thin, but I had to humble myself and obey what was spoken.

The church service was over. I got my babies; I didn't fellowship with anyone. I got to my car and while taking the back-way home, the devil got in my thoughts. *You aren't worth it, no one loves you, you might as well kill yourself, nothing is going to change you, will stay in pain, no one cares.* I began to agree with the devil; adding on saying, *you might be right. I'm tired of living* and tired of being in this dead church, tired of sacrificing, tired of sowing seed not seeing any results, tired of hurting.

I began to swerve the car all over the road. Mind you, we are on the lonely backroad with no vehicles. Just us. If I kill us all, no one will find us. I started speeding up, and I was getting ready to run right into a ditch when Zion said, "Mom, I love you."

I came to my senses QUICKLY!! I slammed on the brakes extremely hard as the car was just inches from the ditch. I put it in reverse to get back on the road and pulled over as I was screaming, JESUS I NEED YOU. I hung down my head, gripping the steering wheel and crying. I could hear over my crying, from the backseat, my daughter said softly, "Mom, you're going to be okay. Take us home so you can get some rest."

I cried even louder. I sat there as God began to speak, saying: "You have purpose. The devil has been trying to take you out since your mother's womb." And right there in the car the bible had flipped over on the floor and a strong wind began to blow the pages. When I picked up the bible, there was Job Chapter 10. My eyes landed on verses 19-22 which read:

I should have been as though I had not been: I should have been carried from the womb to the grave; Are not my days few? Cease then, and let me along, that I may take comfort a little; Before I go whence I shall not return even to the land of darkness and the shadow of death; A land of *darkness, as darkness itself; and of the shadow of death, without any order and where the light is as darkness.*

I'm reading, and my mind is just out of it until God began to minister to me; allowing me to hear his small, still voice.

"In the season of your life, as the word reflects on you as an unborn and being born right now. The devil had an assignment to kill you. He used drugs and alcohol for your mom so she could cope from not wanting you and abusing substances to harm you. She was so unsure about whether or not to keep you. She couldn't cope with life, so she tried to take your life. I had my hands around you during her pregnancy with you because I knew she was birthing a "Gifted Miracle." You should have been carried from the womb to the grave, but I was there with you. I have to use your kids to keep you on track. Listen to them anytime they say anything. Don't take it lightly but heed it, grasp it, hold on to every word that flows from the babes' mouths while you are in a very dark place. They are your light overshadowing death to keep you alive for destiny that awaits you. They protect you also and heal you with their words alone."

Wow, was all I could say. In a complete daze, I drove off with a sound mind and was ready to tackle the world with what was deposit into my spirit from God and the encouragement of my daughter.

I received a few extra days on my job, so I was working a full week. I was at home preparing myself for what lies ahead, even though I was on the edge because graduation being so close. I was very nervous and excited to be walking across the stage. I walked around the house trying to get our things together, but because I have such a short attention span, I moved to another task before finishing the one I had started. I pondered, concerned about how I would finish writing my book(s), about work, being effective in church, plus the boatloads of work that came with single motherhood. I got lost in my thinking because all of this was just too much to handle (in my mind).

My life seemed to be flipping. Again, I started to doubt God and totally forgot what he promised me. It got so bad that I was just floating with no oxygen through life. I didn't even understand how I was breathing. All the fire I had for God was gone. I started to do things my way. AGAIN. What was so scary about that was I could go back to the old me with no hesitations! No inhibitions!

Dinner was cooking and the aroma from the food had the house smelling good. As I did a 'million' things at once, I somehow, forgot to pray before we ate our dinner. I was in total burn out mode and my stomach was full from eating a great meal. I fell asleep instantly. I began to dream the minute I closed my eyes:

Life was complicated. There were roses falling from the throne; dying turning from red to black as they blew away. They turned into ashes and the ashes spread into a word on the grass. The word was HELP with an acronym (H)abits (E)rupted (L)eeching (P)eople. The word vanished. I'm standing there confused, can't find my way in the warning. I'm crawling, looking for this word and it's not there. I see God reaching for my hand. I'm trying my best to get to him. The struggle of me pulling causes me to fall. I fell and missed his arms of protection. So now I can't tell him all about my problems. I'm lost and I never got to God.

Suddenly, I felt Zion shaking, me saying, "Ma, it's time to get up. You got to get to work."

I smiled at her as my heart was racing. I started rushing, trying to prepare for the day ahead of us. I abhorred being late for work. I got on board; got focused on what I needed to do, still making it to work on time.

I clocked in and checked to see what was on the day's agenda. I remembered there was something important that I had to do for me. I picked up the phone and called Ms. McHover, informing her about graduation practice and that I needed to take off. She insisted that I finished up as much work as I could, and resume work the next day. I was filled with so much joy; finally graduating and getting a college degree. I thought to myself,

Crowned Butterfly

I'm graduating in life, growing in God, growing in my spirit, growing as a mother, growing as a woman, and growing in my writing.

I was almost at the finish line; just hadn't crossed over yet, I still had some more stages to walk before getting to who I needed to be, and that is okay. God is going to see me through because what I long for will be my reward and I shall rejoice someday.

I finished up my paperwork and tackled the last two classrooms. Yes, cleaning is so therapeutic for me. It clears my mind and my thoughts flow smoothly. However, there was dust settled everywhere. I blew on the dust and as it faded away, the spot that was dusty looked new and improved. God said to me in a small still voice, "Daughter as spotless as you have these areas where dust was placed, I'm about to blow on some things in your life making it clean for you. It's so much unwanted (dust) attached to you.

Opportunist that see you are steady trying to cling because you are about to prosper. Some see money, some see you as a helper. They don't need you but want to add more on to what they already have because they know you will do it; placing more stress and burdens on you to keep you drained and distracted. Beware in this season."

My phone vibrated and startled me away from my moment with God. It was an EX calling. Luckily, I still remembered the number, so I just looked and laughed. I was being tested from that very word that

31

God had just spoken to me. My supervisor called me to the front, and I ran quickly, asking her, was everything okay? She said yeah, and asked if I wanted to be a key holder to open the building at 6:00 a.m. Without hesitation, I said yes. I thought this could be more income, and I wouldn't have to worry about my needs being met. I took the offer. I found out that one of the employees had quit for whatever reason and the door that was closing for her was slowly opening for me. If that makes any sense.

I hadn't been at the job that long and SUDDENLY I received a promotion. Now, I open the building and did the secretary work. I soon came down off the high saying, OH SNAP!! How will I write my books? How will I do this? How will I do what God had assigned to me. God said this is going to be hard on you adding a lot of stress. I humbled myself interceding back with him. *God what is it you want me to do, because I don't want to mishandle my assignment and abort my will?* He gave me the amount of eight months to continue on to work there (that number represents NEWNESS). I said Okay Lord. I will obey.

Diving back into my work and not keeping up with the time, I forgot it was my lunch break so instead of eating I begin to write. I was sitting writing a poem called "There Is a Pit So Deep" and the part that ministered to me had my spirit uplifted and (I hope it blesses you too)!

Crowned Butterfly

Stay strong yes it gets rough
Stand firm you must hold on.
There is a pit so deep
You finally gave in surrendered
Giving it to God
This time you reached and climbed
You were able to be pulled up
God saw how hard you tried,
He gave you the mercy and grace
To be free to repent to be saved.

Chills went through my entire body because that line of poetry hit home for me. It replenished me. As I heard the other employees come in, I hurried to close my folder. I'm very protective of my writing, plus God was still hiding me, and he was not ready to bring me forth or talk about it. I was still being equipped for a lot of stuff.

One of the employees asked. "Skyye what are you writing?"

"Oh, just writing. It makes me free."

Then they switched the conversation.

I'm saved but still finding myself in Christ. My lifestyle has evolved just a little from worldly things to Godly. I still had struggles, but I maintained the best I knew how. They begin to talk more, and my ears couldn't handle all that was being said by mouth. I exited the room; going where it was peaceful, protecting my spirit and more importantly, respecting my walk with God. I sensed that they may have thought I was acting 'funny,' stuck up or whatever but I wasn't. I was staying in my rightful place as I was becoming the Woman of God that I was being shaped and molded into and a grieving spirit is not what I needed. I had to stay focused on God as he was growing me up to be what he created me to be. I'm in a place where I have to let the fire burn for God even while it's leaving. I still operate off the little I do have, and hearing from him a little more. His voice was beginning to get clearer as I sat in the quietness to intercede with him. Sometimes it takes the ungodly to show you who you are in Christ; can it be a little uncomfortable? Absolutely, but I knew I was a light to them that shined through their darkness no matter what took place. I never went out of character. I kept it Pure, Just & Holy, being an example and shining for Jesus.

The break was over so I got myself back to work finishing up all that I needed to finish up so I could go home. Excitement took over my body as I thought about the next day. "GRADUATION PRACTICE" I'll be a college graduate in four more days. It seemed unbelievable. As I sat there in a daze just thinking of the goodness of Jesus, all I could do was smile. I snapped out of it to get back to my tasks. The kids were down napping, so it was so quiet. As they napped, I cleaned some more to keep my mind clear and while doing so I overheard my coworkers talking and the subject matter was a bit much. As they continued talking, my spirit started to feel so vexed because what they were speaking on was soul ties and addiction to sex, which I was being delivered from. In fact, I was practicing celibacy and I didn't think I would get as far as I did, BUT GOD! However, I'm battling in my mind, should I say something or mind my business. The Holy Spirit took over and I began to speak on my experiences, sharing a little but not too much. I was in the midst of writing my story and they were encouraged and amazed. At the same time, they were very anxious about this book that's in route because they were like, *You did that. You look so innocent.* I could tell they were a little confused but was inspired as well. Once I shared that God had put a joy in me, I couldn't even explain. I felt free knowing that God was using me a such a young age. After I ministered to them, I walked away, praying those spirits off me. I was burden loaded with heaviness.

It was close to time to go home. I got everything done, so I was able to help with the kids, basically just getting familiar with the whole process of childcare. After I finished helping, my supervisor let me off an hour earlier because of graduation practice the next morning. I got my kids from their classrooms and got in the car, so we could get home. Before pulling off, I noticed my phone. I had received a lot of messages from my exes (Another Test), and just men in general. It seemed as if they can smell when you are single. The minute you get focused, here come the distractions. I was curious to hear what they were talking about. Yes, I surely was. I had just ended an engagement. I figured I needed a friend, but it was too soon for all that. I had much more healing to do so I left all that alone. I had entered into a new world. I know it may not seem like a big deal on the outside looking in but imagine your own path of trying to find yourself and keep yourself as a saved woman. The easy part is getting saved. The hard part is staying saved. At one point, I was just a believer and not knowing the difference until now as I walk on this journey of living for God. All things considered, you still can slip because I did.

I needed a few items before going home, so I went to the store. I ran into Jerimiah who I went to high school with. He was an employee at the store. He spoke to me and I spoke back, and the conversation carried on, which I didn't inspect or discern but the talk was interesting. It was getting so good I had to cut him off because I knew I had to get home to do my motherly duties. I told him that I wasn't trying to be rude, but I really have to go. My phone rang, It's my aunt asking if I was still going to church. I told her I was unsure because I had to prepare for my graduation practice that I had the next morning. I hung up the phone, and

God spoke to me instantly saying, "Go" and I'm like, "But God," laughing at myself for questioning God. Who am I.? I didn't want to go to church. The more I thought about it, the more my mind got tired of fighting whether I needed to attend service or not. Moreover, my body started to pain. OMG! My body was under a severe attack, but I was pushing through the tiredness.

We made it to the house, and I got everything in order for the next day. While preparing something quick for the kids, God spoke to me again, saying, "Take your Sunday school bag."

I said, "Huh? Why God? This doesn't make a bit of sense."

God said, "Do you trust me?"

"Yeah, sometimes, but at the very moment I'm confused." I obeyed nevertheless, going into prayer because I felt so sick and in all that, my spirit kept alarming loudly, *Pray for Devon.* I'm the one that needs to be praying for myself.

After I finished praying, I grabbed my car keys, gathered the kids, and our belongs to get in the car and the car it wouldn't start. I'm thinking *OH NO!* I'm getting furious with God saying, "God, you told me to do these things and now this. Why is all this stuff happening to me?" Tears were forming but being released on the inside because I had to stay strong for my kids. I could not and I would not let them see me break. I calmed all the way down. "God, I'm sorry. I'm coming to you with a repentance heart. Please forgive me for acting out of character." I took a deep breath still trying to get the car to start. I had no other choice but to call my aunt for a ride to get to church.

She came and we were on our way and down the street when we ran into an accident. The same street I take all the time to get to church and I'm sitting in the back of the car saying over and over that could have been my children and me. "God, thank you for sparing us." I just couldn't stop thanking him. I became so humbled.

See, sometimes God can get our attention in the strangest ways when we don't understand, he is there protecting us. So, there I stood there just in between two situations but on the verge of a whole new way of thinking. The indescribable thing about God is that he never gives up even when we are trying to find our own way. He knew I didn't belong on the road and I'm so grateful God saved me.

I walked into the church and I saw kids. God took me back to Sunday when no one showed up. They all came to bible study. So, the lesson I prepared didn't go to waste after all. I got a chance to teach when the pastor gave me permission to pour into them as I did. After receiving the lesson, the children went before everyone in bible study to tell what they had learned as God gave it to me to give to them. I was in awe. My heart was bursting open with joy. I love youth. In fact, I have a very big heart for them. See, I had to fight my way to my assignment. The devil tried to cancel me, BUT GOD!!

Whewwww, he kept me going so I could see what was ahead of me and at that point, I asked, "God, help me to understand that you know all things. Take completely over my mind so I won't waver or go in a different direction."

It was time to go home. I pulled out my phone and saw a weird number had called 20 times. I wasn't certain if I should call the number back. I thought it might be a bill collector. My mind was so blown how God used me. I was still stuck on the fact that he chose me to be a vessel. My aunt interrupted my thoughts. The car stopped and I realized we had made it home. I could relax and rest in God. All duties were done. It was extremely late, and I drifted off to sleep, exhausted from all that had taken place that day.

Life has a way of showing you different things you have to face while being strong at the same time in your weakness. Not knowing how the weather can strangely appear as you can't always be protected from the cold of life. The circumstances may hit hard because you're not sure when God will blow, but sooner or later, the storm will be over.

Morning arrived and I was overly excited. Since my car didn't start the night before, I called to see if my cousin could take me to graduation practice. He agreed to take me with no problem. He told me he was on his way so while I waited, I noticed my phone lighting up with no sound. I had it on silent while at church the night before. It had been ringing silently constantly. I didn't answer because I felt like if I had answered it, I would have been late and I love to be on time, so I sat there. My cousin made it and was blowing the horn for us to hurry along, and we headed out the door.

We were on our way to Clarkdale, Mississippi. As we rode, as always, we had so much to talk about in deep conversation about life, laughing, talking, joking just enjoying the ride and one another's company as family. The ride was so smooth and soothing. FINALLY!! We make it to the college. I was so nervous but so happy too ☺ We walked into the building, and it dawned on me that I was about to be a college graduate. As the instructions were giving out, we had to do what was told so the program could go smoothly. We lined up to practice how we would walk in and out. We positioned ourselves to turn to our chairs, walking down the row where we were placed to sit. The minute I sat down; I heard my phone vibrating in my purse. It was the same strange number, so I was curious. I bent over, whispering hello, hello. "This Devon. I'm in jail."

Immediately, I left practice, rushing out the building asking him what for? He said, "I can't talk long, but I want to apologize; asking of your forgiveness and to say I love you."

I said, "You know what? I don't have time for this foolishness."

He said, "Well, my time has expired to talk to you over the phone."

I replied, "Mine just did too," ending the conversation with, "God bless you."

I walked back into practice with a vexed spirit. My excitement was gone. I felt so lost and at that point, tired of dealing with everyone else's problems. Walking into something so severe but leaving out sore. "God, when will I get out of this bondage, the burdens, and the brokenness. I'm breaking God, I need you to repair me. Where are you?"

I went into the restroom and God spoke to me, telling me to open my bible. I didn't have one by hand, but I had the app on my phone, just in case. I scrolled to Habakkuk 3:17-18 "Although the fig tree shall not blossom, neither shall fruit be in the vines; the labour of the olive shall fail, and the fields shall yield no meat; the flock shall be cut off from the fold and there shall be no herd in the stalls: Yet I will rejoice in the Lord, I will Joy in the God of my salvation."

God said to me, "Don't take it strange that you feel stagnant in this season for I am preparing and placing you into something new, something different, something miraculous. As you flourish on dry things, you will blossom from the rut of the oil you carry. You are in the wilderness and this is the time to rejoice. As you do so, I am going to give you the strength to endure what you thought would not bring fruit to your suffering of labor."

Chapter Three

Milestones

"Deep sigh!" I was trying to wrap my mind around all that had just happened. Life was draining me. I had to get back to graduation practice. We did one more practice to finalize everything. My mind was racing; going faster than a race car sliding from side to side on the racetrack, trying to reach the finish line. But my thoughts weren't finished. They continued on the race. I was ready to go home, go to sleep, and sleep the day away; knowing I couldn't do that. So much for wishful thinking, though. I had to attend to my kids, plus start my new shift from six in the morning until closing at 5 o'clock. A full day. Silently I said, "God, all I ask is that you be with me because I don't know how I will pull this off every day."

My cousin texted me, letting me know he was outside. When I got to the truck, he was on his phone, and we really didn't talk much. To be honest, I was kind of glad. I didn't have any words anyway. I was completely numb the whole ride back; silenced from the pain that was added to existing wounds while in the midst of my stumbling blocks, and trying to lean on my own power and be sensitive to the spirit. I learned to face issues and reflect in the moment, trusting God for the life he extended to me.

These milestones had me wandering on a bumpy paved road that never seemed to smooth out. I asked God, *why me? Are you sure?*

He spoke to me, "There are more stones that will be thrown your way. I know you can handle the hits; that's why I chose you, even while traveling a mile to complete the assignment."

There are times when we don't know what to do or how to do it and God will show up with the answer we long for.

We made it back to Cleveland. I stopped by the daycare to pick up the kids. As soon as I entered the door, my supervisor was handing me the keys and giving me the security code to the building. I smiled, said, "Thank you, see you tomorrow."

When I got home, my mind was still a wreck - a complete crash. I got the kids settled so I could get some quiet time. I started writing, hoping to be free. I got so far out of my mind that I sat in the computer room, beating myself upside my head. My mind was in a very dark place, and as I participated in spiritual warfare of not knowing who I was, my identity began to sink deeply. I cried! I screamed! Doing it repeatedly. I didn't know what was going on with me. My spirit was vexed. My body was anxious. My phone rang countless of times and I didn't want to pick up. It was the pastor and I was in no position to talk. I pulled myself together quickly answering. She began to minister to me and what she was saying wasn't sticking because I didn't receive it. I listened but I just wanted whatever was going on with me to go away. She started to talk a little more, saying God had two assignments for me. I'm like, *I'm swamped, I have all this other stuff I'm doing.* But I humbled myself as she continued talking. She told me that I could do it and don't give up on what God is trying to do through me; very encouraging to say the least. But I was battling in my mind. She began to pray. Afterwards, she said, "I need you to write a poem for Sunday and the next few months my son's church is having a youth revival. I want you to give them an encouraging word through poems or however you are willing to write for the youth. You are already on the program and you have plenty of time to come up with something creative."

"Thank you, Pastor," I said as I ended the conversation. *Now, I can't back out of this.* In all honesty, I'm a very shy person. Staring in the faces of other people is not one of my strong suits. I will fallout LOL. But where much is given much is required right?

I was feeling better, just a little, so I was trying to figure out what I would write for Sunday. God gave me something within seconds:

The 3 T's (Time, Transitioning & Transparency). I was writing and as God downloaded it to me. I poured it all out on paper, and as I read over the poem, it really ministered to me.

Not realizing, night fell with none of my duties accomplished, and I was up half of the night. I couldn't sleep; it was 2 in the morning. I checked my Facebook, and I'd received a message from Zed. I in-boxed him back and we exchanged numbers. With all I had going on, I really didn't need the distraction, but I allowed myself to get involved anyway. We texted until it was time for me to go to work. I stopped because I knew I had to be attentive to my kids' needs and get us already for a long exhausting day. When everything was in order, we walked out the door to the car, heading to the daycare, which was just two minutes away.

I had my gospel music playing at the daycare, setting the atmosphere with prayer. I also gave the center a fresh smell with my favorite watermelon candle, before the parents started flowing in. I opened the door every morning at 6:20 a.m. I was with all the kids until 8:00 a.m. when the time came for me to switch roles from the key holder to the secretary.

My phone vibrated in my pocket. It was Devon texting me with foul language because I'd been rejecting him. This was not the season for mess; I just blocked him and carried on with my day. With all the distractions, I'd soon to lose focus. Well, with the route

I was taking I had already let the enemy of distractions in. Please don't forget that our enemy hates us and will steal every ounce of joy he can away from us. But the most confused Christians are those who live with a foot in both worlds. They hedge and gamble with life, having one eye on heaven and one on earth. They call on the name of Jesus, but they still try to find that sense of security, satisfaction, pleasure, or fulfilment from the world. They are riding the fence, hoping to not scratch anything; afraid of the great 'yes' because they are not happy. I was in that very place. A real place that could either hinder my walk or help me excel to my destiny. But as you can see, I had rerouted, trying to dodge God but ended up shipwrecking.

At work, I performed my usual: answering calls, filing receipts, and papers, trying to get my mind to ease into a state of relaxation and calmness. Work did it for me. I can't run from everything, but it will eventually chase me right back down in my own home. I was always free at work, although no one ever knew anything was going on with me because I would smile all day. I found that place to escape since the school could no longer do it for me. This was going to be a long rough week but well worth it because I would be graduating in three days, walking the stage, getting my Associates in Arts Degree. I was in awe and went into worship because of the goodness of Jesus. The phone rang and interrupting my praise, so I had to stop praising. It was Mrs. McHover calling to see how I liked opening and to congratulate me on graduating soon. I couldn't wait to get off the phone to thank God over and over. "Whewwww" was all I could say. I came back to earth off that spiritual high to get back to work before naptime and my clean up time hit.

Jaden called my phone, but I missed his calls. I texted him he said he wanted to see Jabari, he wants to come around more, and I'm like, "Yeah right! Why, all of a sudden?"

He said: **Okay... well, I want to marry you. I think we should give this relationship thing a try**.

I'm sitting and staring at the message. I couldn't reply, so I go into deep thought trying to convince myself that I may need this, but who am I kidding. I'm in the process of starting a relationship with someone now. This can turn out very good or go very bad. I find myself going back into my old ways.

Oh, my distraction #2. I gave in texting him back, saying **Yes, we can start something new being that we never got a chance to build; we might can be a family someday.** He started to talk with some sense. Everything he was saying was beautiful and loving. I haven't felt like this in soooo long. It feels good. Maybe this can be something great, but in due time we shall see.

Instead of cleaning, I went to get my coworkers and me some food. As soon as I got in the car, God began to speak, saying: *What you're feeling is temporary. Don't get into this. You're in , of being delivered. You are not all the way there yet. You are still vulnerable, and the void will not be filled to make you whole but to make a deeper hole.*

Now I'm trying to make a decision. Well. Trying to convince God that I need this. Basically, trying to tell him how to write my love story. So, I'm like, forget what I just heard. I will force what I want since I wanted it so badly.

During the whole drive, I'm feeling uneasy. Instead of obeying, I did the total opposite; disobeying what was spoken. I ignored the uneasiness, soothing it by calling Jaden. He talked to me until my break was over. When I returned to the center, I didn't have much time to eat. Too busy laughing and smiling the whole entire time on the phone. My time was up I hung up from Jaden so I could finish up my tasks for the day. The phone goes off again. It's Zed sending this long paragraph, talking sweet too. I smiled all that day. I knew I shouldn't be falling for this stuff, but I couldn't resist what I was feeling from these men even if it's temporary. I wanted to embrace the feeling of being alive, to feel secure in my insecurities.

We all stumble in the same way Eve did when she fell into sin. She knew what not to do, but she did the opposite. On the other hand, as for me, I dug beneath the surface of any sin in my life and found that I was trying to get something good apart from God and his ways. That good thing maybe significance, satisfaction, justice, belonging, comfort, or some physical need, but like always, I tried to get it without God. In the end, it is idolatry. I'm looking at God, but focused on something other than God. (My distractions that is) to only meet my needs and satisfy my desires. These gods promise joy, but they deliver misery and pain. Now I'm on the receiving end of trying to please my sweet Savior Jesus and my sour flesh that never stops rising. I'm being tempted every day. I put my phone away because that is too much action in one day. I was swimming in the head. Whewwww! What a day.

It was time to go home. I needed some milk and a few more items to cook, so I went to the store and ran into Jerimiah again. He said, "Well, well, we meet again. This must be a sign."

We laughed and he wrote his number on my hand, then kiss it. I was like, "Wait now! You are doing too much." He winked at me, saying call him later. Okay so now I'm about to be involved with three men. Man, my flesh is way out of control, but I'm far too gone in this thing now. I left the store, getting everything but the milk, which is what I needed the most. I couldn't risk being late for church. I got home, put my grocery up and headed right back out the door for church service. We had 'healing and deliverance,' and since I didn't have time to change, I just wore my work clothes. I made it there on time as always because

I hate being late for anything. I love to be on time but as usual they were never on time. My kids and I always had to sit in the car to wait for someone to show up to open the door. I'm sick of this, yet and still, I'm being faithful, pressing my way, and giving God what he deserves from me in the most honorable way. I'm sitting in the car and a song came on the radio, "Place of Worship" by William MacDowell; that song wrecked me right there. It ministered to my soul in ways I couldn't imagine, and the part of the lyrics that stuck with me was: *When I'm with you, I'm Free, Free to Worship, Free to bow down, and Free to Shout.*

I have not yet found my freedom. I'm still digging, still wandering in my deliverance, still weeping, still in my mess, and still tripping on God. Want to be free but don't want to let a lot of things go. The song went off and we walked in the church. I instantly get depressed. I didn't feel anything and that became scary for me. I'm asking God right there in church how much longer do I need to stay here. He said, "SOW YOUR WAY OUT" in this season. So, I did as he said, writing what it is I wanted to be free from on the envelope sealing it up with a $100.00.

Service started and I'm just not feeling church. My spirit is so vexed. I wanted to walk out but instead, while praise was going forward, God took me too *Jeremiah 10:19 "Woe is me for my hurt! My severe. But I say, truly this an infirmity And I must bear it."* And

I'm reading it over and over until he ministers to me, but I had to stop reading due to testimony time. Everyone testified but me. the pastor didn't ask me, she told me to testify and I said 'no.' I'm tired of testifying about the same thing. I really don't want to be here but anyhow I'm thankful for being here. I smiled, sitting down to get back to what God gave me in the midst of praise because this word is good.

Now I'm thinking I still didn't understand how a ministry like this will carry on and I have nothing against it, I've just grown tired in every area. I need something new because my excitement for God is on thin ice. I hadn't yet faced an obstacle that required worship nor challenged me to grow more. I was stuck in the same place, not expanding but failing from being so traditional and complacent. Sometimes, I felt the presence of God, sometimes I didn't, but I had so many scars and wounds to offer up to God, I wasn't sure how I would release the pain to be healed from the fear, the guilt, and things I face on a daily. However, in many ways, I understood growing up in church can sometimes feel like a prison of turmoil that you never heal from. "Church Hurt" is the famous word to describe what I'm saying because many churches expect you to conduct yourself according to the "RELIGION" not the "Authority of God's Power," and while you in the position to break religion, you get punished and everything is a sin, having to apologize in front of the entire congregation. While others sit and judge you, while they aren't seen and not heard but you are put on full blast, accompanying shame, trying to hide the pain from the sin you committed. I was the center of attention from not testifying to being open; rebuked in front of everyone, Yes, I was offended! Yes, I was mad, and yes, I felt like it could have been handled in a better way.

Now my dead situation had arisen when she insisted that I repent in front of the congregation for shacking with no ring, living in fornication. Then she gave me the mic to confess. Instead of me obeying what she said these were my exact words: *Devon was the only help I had. I didn't sleep with the church I slept with Devon. God has already forgiven me.*

I guess I was too honest and didn't give the answer she was looking for, so she said I had to stop working in ministry until I'm pure again. I said fine with me, smiled and went back to my seat. Now my scar was enlarged from shame and that situation that was dead, I have to relive; bleeding, non-stop, flowing and leaking in sorrow. I figure that someday I would introduce my story. When I finished making it as cute as me, since I had everything laid out, piece by piece, on how long it will take to get there until I realized nothing included God's will. It was just perfect ideas of a come-up that detoured and delayed my destiny.

I got out of church filled with so much anger. I let the tears flow because I'm thinking and ready to explode from what took place. I'm so furious, I can really do some damage, but I had to instantly ask myself what would Jesus do?

My phone is constantly going off. I powered it off because I'm shutting down and really don't want to be bothered. I'm ready for this week to end. It's too much to bear; mixed emotions, church hurt, work, life, writing these books, these men, and all these distractions that are coming my way. I'm just trying to stay saved with these stones being thrown back to back. But God did warn me there's no need to prep.

I am exhausted mentally but my body is still energized. I want to write. I figured since I'm halfway through with my book(s), it's time to thrive a little harder, but I prayed instead. I was so heavy I drifted off to sleep beginning to dream: "*I'm walking, and a guy comes to me kissing all on me, rubbing and touching me as I pushed him back. He kept getting closer to me being very aggressive. I'm constantly trying to see his face but its blurry. He begins taking my clothes off and I kept saying no. I'm not doing this. I'm saving myself for marriage. He kept bothering me until I gave in. I ended up having sex with him. After we were done, he vanished; leaving me there alone, trying to find my clothes and my way. What did I do? I weep seeking for God. He doesn't answer because I didn't keep my vow of being pure but lost everything for falling into temptation. I'm looking around and no one is there but me., I'm scared, lost, and I can feel God's judgment upon me.*"

The alarm goes off and I jumped. Its 6:20! OOHH LAWD!!! I'm late for work. I'm scrambling trying to get myself together, and the kids. I'm rushing so bad that I went to crank the car up to put all our stuff inside, including the phone, closed the door, and all the locks clicked. I'm like, OMG! Now I'm locked out of the house and the car. I'm so frustrated, I could cry. I can feel myself go into a panic attack, so I'm talking to myself, "Calm down Skyye so you can think clearly."

I ask the neighbor if I could use her phone so I can call my supervisor. I called - no answer. I called my cousin - he picked up and I explained to him what happened - he came right away. I called my supervisor again. She finally answered and I told her what took place. She said she was almost to the center, just get there when I can. The car window was cracked just a little and after struggling for 45 minutes, he got the car door open. I said thank you for always coming to my rescue. Well, what a day to start off my morning. Could it get any worse?

Jesus, I need you in this very hour I'm about to lose my mind. I got to work and discovered someone else had quit so now we are down to three people, and I had to take on the part of being a caregiver, too. My task every day from 6 A.M. until closing was a key holder, secretary, and caregiver, also cleaning up four different areas. So now I'm a caregiver to the infant's room. I took it as a blessing because I'll be able to care for my son a little more because not everyone knew what to do with Jabari. He comes with a boat load of work, to be honest. If it wasn't for God, I would have given up on the kid a long time ago, leaving him in the care of someone else, while I'm Resting In Peace, because there were many days I contemplated taking my life. BUT GOD!! I'm still living.

How am I going to do this? My personal life is a mess, the issues of life are depressing me, these books are causing me more stress and much pressure. I didn't put too much thought into it because I started to feel drained. My supervisor gave me the ends and odds of what to do and what's to come on how to work with infants. This is where God is about to break me. I can't stand to hear a baby cry. It does something to my mental. Not only is this a test, but it's also an assignment. He couldn't have picked a better person for it. (Me of course!) I weigh it out, saying I'm about to quit right now on the same day. There's no way I could do this. God spoke right in the middle of me talking: "No, it's not time to stop, it's time to start. You have work to do. This job is your assignment. Yes, it's temporary. You have a deadline."

I'm interceding back with him saying, "Well. God. You didn't tell me all this would come with it."

He said, "No, because if I had told you; you would abort what I'm trying to birth through you."

"WOW!!!" Was all I could say…. I went on about my workday and it was time to rotate positions, switching roles.

I'm grateful for the opportunity, but I'm trying my best to be strong in my weakness. I had six babies to look after. The first thing my eyes observed is how dusty and unorganized the room was. I had to clean because I couldn't operate in that environment. So being who I am, I reorganized the whole room by myself and had fun doing it too. I had to be comfortable and relaxed. After doing that, and the babies were napping, I prayed and play my gospel music to set the atmosphere according to what I felt in my spirit. I was led to do it. When God places you somewhere, stick it out. The very place he put us, we try our best to run from it not knowing that God is preparing us to be blessed even in our test. And my test begins. All the babies woke up screaming and hollering, lol. I'm whispering, *Lord, give me strength or come and save me in this moment.* I have never experienced so much noise at once, but God helped me through the day. It was his mercy and grace that kept me from spazzing out.

Finally, time for me to go home. My big day is tomorrow. I'm so elated. I got home laid across the bed with tears of joy falling, not because of graduation but because I made it through a terrible week. God kept me in the midst of it all. My phone vibrates and its Asher calling. My eyes are big, and I'm confused. I hadn't heard from him in about four years. Since I didn't answer, he texted me, saying he missed me, and I'm unforgettable no matter who he is with, he would never stop loving me. I'm falling all over him again. It took me back into our college days. That familiar spirit came roaming and well no matter who I conversed with, if Asher said let's get back together, I would drop everything with no warnings, and it was the same with him because of what we had.

The conversation got so emotional and deep, I begin to think that maybe I should drop all these distractions, but I craved for the attention of being wanted and the crazy high I was feeling probably better than any drug: 4 different men, 4 different spirits, 4 different soul ties. Now I'm the "Wild Church Girl" hiding beneath my sin holy by day promiscuous by night; the same routine I acted out in college now just different faces with a different season.

Asher and I stopped texting ending the conversation with we love one another. I begin to clean and my phone rings again. It's Devon. He's back in jail and this time had to do some time for something he did as a teenager. So, I attend to him on the phone; not only that, God insists that I minister to him and encourage him. Then he gave me another idea for my second book. I wrote it down, studied it and went with it. I got off the phone because of the time and I had so much to get done around the house. God spoke again, saying I am going down the wrong road. My Jezebel spirit has taken over and I felt convicted but every time I felt it instead of praying, I would call one of the 4. Crazy, right??

But the feeling I became addicted to is the pleasure. I needed to stay sane even if it cured my loneliness for the moment. I took it all in. I got myself prepared for the next day because I had a long day ahead of me, plus we had to be at the school early. We all got in the bed, and as soon as I closed my eyes, I saw a vision then begin to dream: *"I see my coworker go into a hotel with a man. And as the man led her to the bed, just before they were about to perform sexual encounters, the man's wife, bust in the door, aim a gun at both, shot her husband, and fought my coworker."*

I jumped, pouring in sweat, looked at the time on my phone, and it's 3:00 in the morning. I'm not sure if I should text my coworker what I dreamed or tell her in person because this is serious. I'm so scared, I'm shaking. I typed it all up and couldn't get myself to send it. I deleted. I said God I can't do this, he said you have to tell her whether she receives it or not. Now I feel convicted, I said, well Monday I will tell her. Took a deep breath and got my kids up and ready to tackle the day.

I was so overwhelmed to share my big day with the few family and friends that I invited. They were accompanying me to graduation, which I thought was so sweet and special. I had to meet the pretty lady CJ to get Jabari. She was coming later while Zion, my cousin and I went on ahead to the school, but along the way, I felt so unhappy. It was not enough but I should be grateful and thank God for completing one of the stones that were a lot of miles. I desire and believe so much in myself that better isn't enough, I need greatness. I want to shine a little brighter. My light is still hidden under the tunnel peeping. One day it will shine fully.

We got to the building and it seemed so unreal to be in that very place I had longed for. As the stadium started to fill, I began to get nervous. We walk to the back, line up, and Mrs. Done gave me a hug so soothing it took all my nervousness away. She said I'm so proud of you. Don't stop here, keep going. I smiled standing there in line, waiting and as I ponder on God's goodness, I remembered: before rededicating my life back to Christ, I was pregnant with my daughter and the pastor asked us to bring a picture of our family.

When I got up to the altar, she prayed over the picture of our family. After finishing, she said you hold on and continue to wait in line. I know the waiting seems long but if you be patient for the promise, God will give you your heart's desire. A tear began to fall because now I'm standing, I've waited, and I'm here in one of those places that were spoken over my life years ago.

The line got closer and I was at the door. I'm shaking, I'm uncomfortable, but I can't stop smiling. I finally reach the entrance to walk down the aisle. I felt so good. I'm proud of this very moment because only God knew these milestones that have been paved but stuck and never smoothed out. I kept paving until better came my way. I sat down as commencement went forth and something that stuck out to me of what the speaker said. *Life sometimes detours you, but you can always reroute to get to where you're going.* It was more confirmation so to speak but the scary thing about it all is, I didn't know where I would end up.

As I waited for my named to be called, excitement ring through my body. "Skyye Howze." I smiled so hard. I was so bubbly; tears began to form as I walked across the stage. May 14, the exact same date I graduated from High School, seven years earlier (Completion). I, too, obtained a degree. It still blows my mind to see the miraculous move of God and how his favor reigns on my life. Family and friends were waiting when I got outside. They hugged and embraced me. I left with the pretty Lady CJ. She didn't tell me where we were going, we got in the car and rode out.

It is not about how long it takes, it's about getting it done; but more importantly, getting to your DESTINED PLACE. God's timing is not our timing.

Trust him; wait on him so he can perform miracles as he has done for me.

This day is so overwhelming. We pulled up to our date spot, the Mexican Grill. She knew how much I loved that place. I was so happy and filled with Joy; not only that, I had a big bag of goodies and gifts! We sat down and waited for the food. CJ asks, "How is the book coming along? "I began to pour because I knew if I vented, she would heal me with her soothing and encouraging words. As I always receive and take heed to what she says.

What boosted my spirit up was when she said, "I never saw anyone as strong as you. You are so strong-willed, and your faith is courageous. You are so young, and your drive for life is truly amazing." Since she has seen me at my worse, she knew how desperately I wanted to succeed. Our food came to our table, OMG!! I dived in; I was starving. I thanked God for her and the food. Lol!! CJ has been so great to my kids and me. I love her for being there when I had absolutely no one. She was always there supporting me in everything. Now I'm stuffed and can hardly move.

My phone rings. It's Zion's father calling. I didn't want to answer because we are always beefing, but he just called to say congratulations and keep up the good work. I really wasn't expecting that since we never got along; only agreeing with anything dealing with Zion. Overall, I thought it was nice that he thought of me on my big day. When I got home, I chilled out for the rest of the day.

I really didn't want to go to church on Sunday. I was in a place of growing weary and tired of not growing spiritually. I had nothing against the saints. They helped me grow in the areas I needed to grow in, but I was hungry and thirsty for more. I was dehydrated and needed to quench more of God in this season of my life. Zed texted that he wanted to see me. I was exhausted, so I push it off until the next weekend! I started to get bored. When my mind wanders, it is not good. I begin to write more on my books using the time wisely and not how I see fit, but however long God pours, I will write until he says to stop.

While I wrote, I was closing up my chapter, "Sex Addict." I was so proud of becoming delivered in that area, but the more the distractions came, the weaker I got. My curiosity began to build on being sexual with a few of my 4. I snapped out of it because I felt my flesh rising! I begin to look over my poem for church, the Three T's to God. Instantly minister to me saying those T's are to help you be free. *There will be a time you will be placed somewhere **transitioning** only to be **transparent**. While growing in me, you will grow in the areas you struggle to mature in.*

I sat there mediating on the words that spoke to my spirit. It took me to another place that I really can't explain, but I felt so different. I bent down to pray. I'm so fearful when I'm in front of many but it's my assignment from God. So, whether I want to be bold or not, I have to be. Whatever your gifts and/or calling are, God will see you through what he creates you to do. However, it is true your gift will make room for you but as you are called, the room of manifestation opens up your gift to please God and to help people. God is with you. Please make room for him so your gift can make room for you.

I heard my son coughing uncontrollably. I rushed out of the computer room. He was getting strangled; turning red in the face. I begin to anoint him with oil, praying until I flowed into my heavenly language (what I was taught to do) until his breathing was back to normal. He took one big breath and he screamed so loud that I knew his breathing was back on track. He smiled and chewed on my finger to assure me that he was okay. I kept thanking God over and over. Tears rolled down my face because I'm scared of losing what I birthed but God gets the glory. It's a bit much as I know God is equipping me for a lot of things to come and one day, it will get easier.

I was so tired that I could barely keep focused. I tried sleeping, but I couldn't, and I didn't dream this time. As I dazed, I saw an open vision in my ceiling; the year 2017, and around the numbers were five words floating in between the year - Birth, Patient, Stronger, Levels, and Issues. As I got deeper in my staring, the words faded, dropping like sand, while the numbers dripped in the form of rain. I jumped because as it was falling, it looked as if it was coming down on me. I looked up again and it was gone. I'm so confused; I asked what's up, God? I was still in 2016, I just couldn't understand. I get up, dragging, making myself get ready for church because I pulled an all-nighter and I really do not want to attend. Then this vision of what God showed me is making me ponder so deep until my head starts to hurt.

After sitting for so long, I decided to go church to the same routine, same tradition, same program. There's no excitement. I sit down on the pew, just gazing at the ceiling as the chandelier lights swing back and forth. I see how dim the lights are. The service is gloomy, and my spirit is in mutual agreement. I'm so bored. I just want to get my assignment over with so I can go home.

So, the services took a turn and guess who didn't get to recite her poem? ME!! She, the pastor, went straight into the word. I'm like *Geesh*. Every time I prepare myself for something and obey God, it never happens. I'm sitting in church angry. There's nothing spiritually operating in me at this point. I'm still human, and my feelings are all over the place because I put my all into anything I work on, then when it's time to present it, I'm not able to be a mouth piece for God. It's frustrating! So, I set there in service just lost and ready to go. Tears are falling during service. What am I to do God, when I'm constantly suffering, sacrificing, and losing sleep?

Church service was finally over. I gathered my belongings and told my kids to come on. While leaving out the door, Zion dropped my Bible. I was getting ready to fuss. God said, instead of doing that, just smile and pick up the Bible. It was on 2 Chronicles. My eyes followed the black mark from the ground, taking me to chapter 15, verse 7 which says: ***"Be ye strong therefore, and let not your hands be weak; for your work shall be rewarded."***

I hugged Zion and said thank you for dropping the Bible and she said mommy it was a mistake. I didn't mean to. I said, yes. But the lesson was in the word. She didn't get it but to you, every mistake requires attention from God. He used my daughter to get my attention. He knows how passionate I am about writing. It's truly my freedom and how he uses me just for you! If I would have never gotten the word, I'd say forget these books, but the word ignited my fire and made me write more. So, no matter what flows your way, keep on doing what you are assigned to do in this hour and/or season of your life. Your time will come where you will be rewarded, not from people but from God.

I'm hoping for a smooth week of work because last week was terrible. I'm so tired I really want to call in. I'm not feeling my best. I'm at a point in my life where I'm ready to give up on everything and everybody, including God. Life is taking a toll on me. I feel like I'm suffocating in the middle of the ocean and no one sees me drowning. I'm grasping for air, and in the midst of dying, I need a pause button. But who's going to do it when the ocean keeps waving in dramatic and tragic ways. As I continue on to swim through life, I'm sure someone would rescue me. I truly need saving. One day I will be able to provide for my family without worrying, but right now, I can't afford to quit, plus God gave me a deadline. If I were to just up and leave now, I'd mess up his plan of not only taking care of me but reaching my destiny. It is in the morning and I'm praying about it and moving forward. I tried to go to sleep the night before, but I tossed and turned all night. I ended up pulling an all-nighter - writing, praying, listening to sermons and listening to music, refreshing my spirit and soul; drawing nearer to Jesus.

If my memory serves me correctly, I recall watching a sermon called, "Put Your Phones Down," by Jamal Bryant; basically, talking about distractions of relationships, social media, apps, etc. It was an "Ouch" sermon for me. I was in that very place, being pulled in every different direction, losing focus on what's important to fulfill the lustful desires of being wanted; doing things my way and not God's way.

It was time for work and when I got there, I just wasn't feeling it. I'm dragging the entire time. I sat there waiting for other parents to come and ended up falling asleep from being up all night. I truly was tired and in way too deep of my sleep because I didn't remember hearing a parent coming or calling my name. I jumped and apologized for having them stand there that long without responding. I have to say, I have not gotten used to my routine scheduled yet and there's no need to because as God spoke, I won't be here long. I'm just going with the flow of how God is moving and maturing me along this journey.

The day was not going well at all and I felt in my spirit that it will get worse. I even felt myself getting an attitude. I started to pray right there, leaving no room for the enemy to use me in my thinking. I needed him to shift my mind as I knew he would so I wouldn't take my anger out on anyone, especially the babies. I was caught up on my secretarial work in the office, so I helped around the center. So now I'm in the position to tell my co-worker about the dream. I'm scared and trembling. Taking a deep breath, I really don't know how all this is going to turn out, but I pulled her to the side, telling her what God showed me in the dream. She was just blown away, telling me thank you for obeying. She said, "I have to let you in on something. I do have my bags in the car and was going to the hotel after work, but I'm taking heed to your warning. I'll go home instead."

I'm stuck. My mouth is wide open, but I have no words. I felt the peace of God fill my body. I was happy she received. Most don't. They brush the dream off or have something negative to say. I hugged her and walked off. I just saved her life and a few others because of what God showed me. My other co-worker wanted to get her something to eat, so she asked if I wanted to assist in the room until she got back. I didn't mind at all. I got in there. All the babies were sleeping except for one. She just refused to go to sleep, so I read to her and played with her. I stepped out of the room to use my phone and to use the rest room. I came back to a complete disaster. The baby had pooped everywhere. I said little girl what did you do? I wasn't gone two minutes. She had taken her pamper off, was eating it, and had smeared it on the bed. I had to wash her up and bleach the whole bed. I had never experienced such. That was a wild moment for me, and she just laughed the whole time. I could do nothing but smile and laugh with her. She was the brighter side of my flipped day. But suddenly everything turned so quickly to make matters worse. Jabari got sick with a fever of 100. I gave him some medicine to reduce it until we could make it home.

These attacks are driving me insane. It's only by God's grace, I haven't lost my mind. Jabari's fever got worse. He began to shake as if he was going into a seizure. I just took off for the rest of the day to rush him to the hospital. I'm driving and holding him. How dangerous is that? I plead the blood of Jesus over him as I know how he was in and out losing his wind. I jumped out of the car without cutting it off so they could get him back to normal. They put an IV in him to give him fluids. He was so dehydrated and was going through a relapse from being premature; not adding the fact that in his age bracket and still wasn't talking, eating, not interacting, nor walking. The doctors were shocked that he went that long without relapsing. I wasn't though because I knew the God I served and how he kept my son previously. But the stages of these episodes were very scary, as the doctor agreed with me, walking out to get steroids for his breathing.

I can't fathom all that happening in one day. My baby was so sick, he cried for more than two hours. I laid beside him crying too. I called Mrs. McHover, letting her know what happened and to tell her I would not be back to work until my baby was well. She seemed like she wasn't too excited about that. She asked me so many questions, but I felt she was a little bit to nosey so I cut her off saying my child's health comes first and I'll be back to work when I can get back.

The doctor comes back in saying he had to stay in the hospital for two extra days because of the test results. These are the moments where the quiet times in our situation or life just for that present and brief moment, making it so hard for us to focus on God. Saying, everything will be okay, and then we are afraid to be OKAY because we're anxious and on the edge of what may happen next! Being that the bad is outweighing the good, it causes us to be more anxious to relate the problem, if not, we create the problem; over-analyzing. We don't understand the peace because we are at our most vulnerable in the darkness of discomfort. There's no way we can be filled with joy trying to recover from our distractions of tragedies and issues of life. "Sigh," I just need to breathe.

All my four were reaching out. I only answer for Jaden to let him know that Jabari was hospitalized. We talked more about his health, putting on hold what we were trying to build, making Jabari our main focus. I told him I will give him a call back when CJ walked through the doors. She was actually on duty at work. "My guardian angel" sent straight from heaven. Always present when trouble arises, she gave me a hug and said you can get through this; you have strong faith. She talked more about getting Jabari help and as she loved on him, she says, "I reached out to a therapist in Greenville, MS to further his development skills."

It's time I agreed because he is in a much delayed state. He isn't doing anything, and I'm drained. The crying out in my prayer is paying off. I see God's hand move in the midst of all this. I got on Facebook to clear my mind, but it seemed as if it were more bad things flowing on my timeline than good. I deactivated it until I felt led to get back on. Besides, all the mess I got going on in my life, Facebook should be my last option. I just wanted my son to feel better. I'm lying there can't sleep, can't eat, can't think straight, trying to keep myself in prayer to stay lifted up. I really dislike hospitals and I haven't slept in a day. I pray he get discharged soon.

The doctor came back in saying the test results suddenly changed. He didn't see anything, and he said he wanted to test him one more time. I smiled and said, ok, God. I see you healing my son. The doctor said, "In the meanwhile, Miss Howze, we want to keep doing the breathing treatment, not only here but at home as well, to keep his breathing on track."

CJ called to say she got everything set up for therapy. He starts that following week. I wasn't sure how I would get him to and from Greenville due to my car not running properly so CJ insisted on talking me on her off days and my cousin said he would help as well. If I couldn't count on anyone else, I knew I could count on those two.

Jabari's session would be every day at 12:00 noon. Everything was going so well. The doctor came back and said, "Miss Howze, I don't see anything. I looked and looked. The test results came back well so they will discharge him."

I've miss two days of work plus now since his sessions are every day, I will be back a part time worker. Not only that, the youth day is in about three days. My mental is destroyed. I really need god to shift my mind.

We get home and all I wanted to see is a bed. Zed texted me to see if he could come over. I said sure, maybe it will take my mind off everything. Whatever or whoever can cease my pain, I'll get with it to feel good.

Zed text saying he was outside. I told him to come on in, the door was open. This man was so fine. Lawd, have mercy. Everything I dreamed of. OMG!! I just stared because he was so handsome. At this point, my lust has taken completely over, and I found myself turning into *Curious George*. Now I'm wondering and undressing him with my eyes, but as he got to talking, I didn't miss a beat. I'm tuned into him. We had a lot of things in common. He knew God but not as deep as I did so I didn't beat him up with the word. I just encouraged him of what I knew because I was still growing as well. It was refreshing to talk to someone who understands what you go through without judging you.

As we begin to talk more, he started to kiss on me. I told him no because I was in a place of being delivered as I'm on the journey of practicing celibacy. He said I promised I won't try anything with you, I just want to be intimate with you because I'm into you and want to fall in love with you. I gave in to the "sweet nothings." He started touching my body in ways I never experienced. It felt good too. I know what I'm doing is not right. He began to perform oral sex. Whelp, my vow to God is now in vain and is broken. I feel so crazy. I tried stopping him, but I couldn't resist the feeling. He looked at me saying, Skyye all you've been through, I just wanted you to have some type of release. I got that and a conviction too. I felt so nasty. I know God was not pleased with what just took place. I said, Zed I can't continue on to talk with you because you are causing me to sin and fall back into my addiction for sex. He kissed me, saying ok that's fine, I'll leave.

Satan tempts us to think we can find something good and satisfying away from God, but we must have a strong "No" to anything that promises 'good' without him. The resounding "No" is a great No. The essence of sin is looking for good outside of God and his will, so no matter how it feels, it's not right in God's sight. *God, I just want to do right by you. Please help heal me when I'm lonely.* Just a simple prayer to show him I'm serious.

Before I went back to work, we did Jabari's first session, and it went all wrong. He didn't do anything asked by the therapists. I kept cutting eyes at CJ. She said he's going to do fine. Jabari started to participate then out of nowhere he had a meltdown. All the screaming and crying doesn't do well with my nerves, so I stepped in the room. He crawled to me. He was so happy to see me. He just didn't want to be bothered. All he wanted to do was lay on my chest. That day was pretty rough, but we got through it! I see this process is going to take time, but I know God is going to see me through it!

I became so consumed with trying to figure out a better future that I never checked how these milestones had truly affected me. I didn't realize how hard it was for me until I saw what my son has to go through on a daily. I'm not ready to accept him like this! I try to convince myself that he is normal like other children, but he isn't, so where do I go from here. God, you have to help me through this, if not I will fail as a parent, and possibly give up on my child. So many wandering thoughts because my rush to recovering has never retreated. The load never got lightened. The pain expanded, scattering my wounds wider and wider. I QUIT, I GIVE UP!!! Well I never made it back to work. I stayed off another two days. I had to recuperate. My body was so tense; I could feel the stress move from different parts of my body.

I made it home, took a nap; not thinking my nap would turn into hours of sleep. The night before attending the Youth Revival in Memphis, TN, I had been talking to Zed. I started falling for him and as I was sitting thinking of him, he texted me sending me nudes and videos. I was so tempted to send him pictures of my body as well, but I couldn't build my nerves up to do it. Just looking at what he was sending had me wanting to call out and get with him. I had already sinned, breaking my vow of "purity," so I might as well do more. I was holding up strong though until he started sending me links of porn sites. It got so interesting. I began to touch myself. I'm like, Lord, you know I'm not quite delivered from these porn sites. Every time I reach a level where I thought I was truly delivered, I'm reminded all over again that it was just buried, and not rooted out of me. Just as I craved for the feeling of pleasure from watching someone else get busy, I ended right back in that place to get pleased from seeing someone else get what I desired to feel.

So now I'm asking God if Zed is the devil or my test. He didn't respond. I continue to watch the porn site and found myself masturbating. Once I finished, a conviction came over me so heavy, all I could do was cry, and because I knew what I did was wrong. Plus, I had to minister the next day. I had to repent and cry out all night to get back in alignment with God because I didn't want to get before God's people unclean and everything to be in vain.

After I was purged, I texted Zed and told him I couldn't converse with him anymore. We had to drop this. He said he will come over to talk. I said that's not a good idea, I have church tomorrow. He said he still will show up. I didn't text back. I ignored the message, laid there until I drifted off to sleep. I woke up so refreshed, I felt brand new and thanked God for his new mercy and his great grace to get things right. I got up to get us ready to head out to Memphis. I traveled with one of the minsters from the church. I was so uncomfortable; I do not like sitting for long periods of time. I stared out the window the entire ride. When I know God is always there, the purposeful time gives me an awareness of his sweet presence; mainly the assurance that he will be there all day long. I'm in total silence, mediating, keeping myself in good spirit and excited, but nervous about sharing what God has given me to give his people. As I closed my eyes and open my ears, God said open your bible to Ecclesiastes, Chapter 6. I read the whole chapter. Four phrases that he had me to focus on out of the scripture were: *untimely birth, depart in darkness, labor of man,* and *vexation of spirit.*

As I let the words stir my spirit, he said: *My child, something has been laid up prematurely. An untimely birth is going on in the spiritual realm. Pain is wrecking the souls of many people even as for you, who's trying to deliver what God wants them to fully carry. They are so eager to get the word out, but it's not ready to be pushed out. Depart from the darkness of what's trying to kill what's inside of you. Yes, I have you to speak but that's not it. You have more to release; you have to protect it at all cost. The labor of man is not in vain. What should have killed you is only making you stronger. The vexation of your spirit is to alarm and alert you; warning you from all evil that's trying to take away what I'm birthing in you. I am the head of your life; the time is now to carry FULL as you walk in this season of place with me.*

OMG! That was so powerful. I received every word that was sent from Heaven. Hearing God's voice always kept me in line. I drifted off to sleep, waking up to someone shaking me.

We had made it to the church late. I was supposed to be at the top of the program, and it was close to the end of the program. As soon as I got in the door they called me up. I'm sweating because I don't understand how I fit in. Why God is constantly using me every time I fall in error? I've always used my shyness to escape from being used, but do I have any other choice? I'm standing where God placed me, and I still wasn't sure what I had to offer. I took a deep breath, eyes glued to the wall, looking straight ahead, I begin to open my mouth reciting my poem called:

YOUTH
"The Youth are very important
But we always seem to go unnoticed,
Our God is ready to save us all
To be a Light to this dying world,
Understand that the Christ is for you,
It's to give God everything you got
So, don't be afraid let God have his way
He's watching, he's waiting
To grab a hold of your young souls
To cleanse you so you can be free
To walk in victory
And to make a smooth transitioning

Crowned Butterfly
Into your Destiny"

The fear I had gone away, and everyone received what was said. They ended it with a clap as I walked off. The MC of the revival said to me, my God, that was very encouraging, young lady. Keep up the good work. Walking away from the stand, I felt so free just to let someone else hear my words besides me saying it over and over or recording myself.

The Guess speaker from Columbia got up to preach, and he started talking about how when he first got saved and how he struggled with masturbation, porn, and being an addict to sex to satisfy the flesh. I'm in the pews cringing biting my nails because that's the same struggle I'm trying so desperately to get delivered from. I was saying "Ouch." That word was tearing me up. Tears began to fall; it was a very real place for me and pointed me out right where I was sitting, calling me to the front.

He called everyone up to the altar. Before he got to me, he started to lay hands on people. A mass deliverance took place. The spirit was high, and God was on the move. After he was done, he stepped back in my face, started to prophecy, saying: "You don't have to be ashamed about what you are coming out of. We all have struggles. The devil tried to keep you at home, but I'm glad you came."

I'm balling in tears when he said, *you have a lot of greatness that lies within you. You have to stop running and let God use you. Hold your hands up. He touched my hands* and my God, my God, I felt the fire of God go all through my hands. He said, *the exhortation you spoke for the youth was just the beginning; your prayer life must go to the next level. I see God using you in mighty ways because of how your spirit travels. You breathe life, not only into the young but old as well. You will be performing the "Gift of Healing" with your hands and words. You are about to become a writer that speaks to the world, not just one individual.*

October 24, 2016 – three year later, and this prophecy still sticks to me.

When we got back on the road, there's no way I could sleep. I stayed up because for one, I was still high in the spirit from church, and secondly, due to me not liking to travel especially at night my eyes were glued to the road, so as we traveled, I'm thinking about life decisions and how can I become better in God. That prophecy gave me a lot of confirmation. My mind is actually still blown; I can't even fathom what I heard. It was all accurate. It gave me a peace that syringes my heart on every end, but to pass the time on the road, I listen to music to keep my spirit at ease and to keep my eyes on Jesus.

God insists that I mute the music, speaking to me, telling me to turn my bible to Matthew 5:41 and it read: ***"And Whoever Compel you go one mile, go with***

him two." *Go the second-mile. Daughter, it's the extra mile you have to go even when no one is watching you, or even if they are watching, keep the spirit of excellence because you set high standards in me. Your life gives me praises. Every time you are used, you are honoring me. Others are watching your life; they are watching how you live as you represent me. Do more than what's required, and you will see my goodness and favor in new ways you can't grasp.*

Man, oh man, God is working on me. At this point, I feel like I'm floating. We finally got home. I'm EXHAUSTED! I haven't been to sleep in two days. I got the kids settled in, fed them, and as for me, I was already full off of all that took place. I just wanted to rest the night away in God. Food wasn't needed; as I got comfortable in his arms, I fell into a sweet sleep, beginning to dream: *"I am walking. I see old college students I went to school with. They begin to talk to me, and I see a few of my exes. They started chasing after me. What was a full fun day of events, soon turned into a complete disaster. Some people came to the campus to check everywhere, and it was a man and a woman sitting. As they search each person to rob, I put my money in my bra, and after that they disappeared. Now I see nothing but women with guns spraying chemicals that burns your skin off. So, they are killing everyone on campus, they head for me, shooting at me.*

As I run with so much fear in my heart, I run into Asher. He laid there comforting me; as he placed his face on my face, he kisses me. We cuddle; almost hit it off with sex until the shooting started again. I jumped. He said. Skyye,

81

don't run, I'm here to protect you, but I ran again. They were aiming to kill me. I wouldn't die. I ran every time they shot. I went back to get my money after I realized it was missing. The woman said I took it out of your bra. That was all the money I had, screaming at the woman. She said, I needed it, so I stole it. So now I'm pondering on how I will make it. The shooter managed to kill everyone on campus.

They were still after me, trying to kill me. I'm hiding, I'm ducking. They sprayed acid on me. I ran down the street, and I ended up at a car wash. The shooter saw another shooter telling them to take me out. He shot at me, he chased me, he couldn't catch me, and he finally shot me in the leg. I'm still running. I grab one of the cars. It was on empty. I still drove it. The man shot the car up. I made it home. I was so scared, but I was safe. They killed everyone on campus; left them dead, while I'm still alive. I still had life."

I woke up so confused. God what are you trying to tell me? WHOOAAA SMH. I didn't ponder too long, and I know God will give me the revelation later.

I had to minister again, reciting my poem I was assigned to write. I still feel good from last night, so I shook it off because God is yet about to use me. I'm getting ready to head out the door for church but before I leave, I take the trash out that was sitting in the house for two days. Something fell out of the bag, and as I turned around to pick it up, I hear glass shattering into pieces - flying in the house - big chunks of it. I turned around heart beating fast but thanking Jesus at the same time because if I had never turned around, I would have been cut up bad! I'm like Lord; this devil really doesn't want me to open my mouth. He has been causing so many distractions, and this one shocked me the most. He really wants to harm me, and his mission is to kill me, so I won't see purpose. The glory may be rocky, but it's worth fulfilling so keep pressing through the attacks.

I ran to tell my landlord what happened, and she was pissed, so I left her and headed straight to church. I didn't let what happened to stop me from going to church. As I was driving, God said, keep pulling and pushing. I held on that all day, got to the church, and I felt a heaviness come over me out of nowhere. Okay, God, you got to help me. I know there's nothing wrong with me. He said, *yes you are right, but it's a few people need your words but be in prayer before you get up to read what I have given you.* I did what was instructed. It was my turn to go up there and as I read, I felt the shift as I shared with the people. I would also like to share just a portion of my poem The 3 T'S:

"Yes, we all have a destiny to be fulfilled,
But until we (you) endure the pain
You will never see the forthcoming of your purpose.
When you stop trying to do things as you planned,
You will never see god's plan flow for your life.
The destination isn't far.
It might be cloudy and foggy along the way,

Skyye Howze

But keep wiping your tears it's soon will turn into joy,
The hurt, the disappointments, and brokenness it's about
to fade.
Keep traveling although it's bumpy, keep moving
God is right there with you, in fact, he's in your lane
Your purpose is to be served out of pain,
And your destiny is to be fulfilled out your praise."

I felt so good. Not only did my heart receive my own words, but their hearts did too. And I hope you grab hold to these encouraging words as well. ☺

After finishing up, I had to leave. I was invited to dinner. I didn't stay long but out of respect, I showed my face and brought my gift. I had to go to work the next morning and catching up on my rest was all I needed to do. My body was shutting down. I got home, powered my phone off, and went straight to sleep. I didn't have the time or energy to be bothered with anyone.

My daughter came in the room. As she was shaking me, I looked at her with my eyes half open and then looked at the time. "Gosh, it's 2'clock in the morning."

She said. "Mom, I threw up in my sleep."

I jumped up quickly. She was extremely hot. I didn't check her temperature because I knew she had a fever. I gave her medicine, and she crawled in the bed with Jabari and me. She got in my arms. I prayed over her and myself back to sleep.

The alarm went off. I'm sitting on the side of the bed dragging. I got on up, put on my work clothes and went back into the room. Both of my babies were up and silent, not saying a word, but both were whining. That's not normal because they are very free-spirited and happy babies. I touch them both again, and they were so hot! I checked them with the thermometer, and they were both running a fever of 102! I dropped everything to rush them to the hospital. I'm fumbling carrying both of them, trying to get them in the car, and trying to keep it all together while being helpless and trying not to break , all at the same time.

My mind was in a million places. I got them to the Emergency Room. The nurses came in to check blood. Neither kid likes needles, so both of them were hollering. I'm fighting the tears back because I have to be superwoman, but my cape is slipping off. I smiled and began to coax them through the pain. As both babies scream, one nurse said, "Ma'am, how do you do it?"

I simply replied, "Jesus. He carried me and held me up through the whole process." One had an ear infection and one had a stomach virus.

After getting discharged, I got in the car, tears begin to fall, and so did my cape. I was breaking, and I believe God was stripping me too! I got home and got them into bed. I went into an awful episode of depression, wanting to commit suicide. I'm ready to take my life and my kids' lives, too. I'm screaming and falling all over the floor. Having these moments until Jesus freed me from all that was troubling me. I quickly came back to my senses because I needed to live, not only for my babies but for you too.

God, when will all this madness be over? Why do you have us on Earth? I'm tired; I don't see the purpose. Everything is falling apart, and the more I hold on to all that is going on, the worse the falling gets. So now I have to be off work for three more days. My kids are sick; I have to nurture them back to health. I had to get my stress level down too. I never have time for myself, I'm still in the beginning stages of feeling sorry for myself, but at some point, this pity party of emotions has to stop. I'm growing weary and fainting in my thinking. Jesus, I need a touch from you. I have to enjoy me.

You're probably wondering how I would do that with two sick babies? Well, if you must know, my enjoyment is peace and being able to think freely. My quiet time is: **"Venting for Peace"** *There will be times where you will need to be alone, to hear God. He's the calmness to your raging storms. Go deeper in him, and seek him for the unknown pieces of peace. In your time of despair, understand that while you are venting, you are receiving.*

The whole three days of being off, I found the peace I was searching for. My mind was sound, my spirit was full, my soul was refreshed, and I was nurtured back into who I lost during the tragic times of my life.

My time of venting is up. I have to return back to work. We all recovered. God healed us and all things can go back to normal; I hope. I went back to work the next day and felt so out of place. I knew God had done a shift in me because nothing seemed the same. I wasn't going to just up and leave, but I needed some excuse to be released so I can finish writing my book(s). When I got to work, I did my usual routine, and a switch took place while I was out. Now after I open, I get the toddlers, following with the infants in the afternoon. I got on the phone with Jaden. We talked for about an hour, while I was texting Zed and Jerimiah. All three were talking about coming to see me. My eyes begin to get glued to the phone as the topics of our conversations got interesting. I wasn't paying attention to my surroundings. Two minutes later, I fell off to sleep. Don't know how that happened, but someone came in the door. It slammed, I jumped. That is what woke me up. I'm looking around; the room was still in good standards. The kids were watching TV. The owner's daughter, Paige, walked into the room and asked, "Are you okay?"

I said, "Yeah, just tired."

She said, "Yeah, I know." With an attitude, she walked off, so I got on my phone again. This time it was a call about a family matter. I hung up the phone as I heard the supervisor call me to the office. I said, "Yes."

She goes on to say, "Mrs. McHover and Paige saw you on camera on the phone and falling asleep the entire time. She insists that I write you up although I didn't want too because you never do anything wrong, but can you please sign it?"

I said, "Sure," with a smile. I left the office to finish up before we switched rooms. To make time go by faster, I cleaned the toddler room and placed their mats on the floor since it was almost nap time. After the toddlers finished eating, they laid down for nap time. I went in prayer because the peace I vented for was trying to leave me. As soon as I finished praying, I was tested. I was called to the office again. It was brought to my attention that one of the parents was complaining about something that took place in the infant room when I first started in there. I stayed humbled as I could until the parent started to get rowdy. I told her to have a blessed day because I was in no position to argue. Must I add that was my first time in that position, which I am still learning things. Your best out is to be quiet and get out my face because I'm about that life too. When I walked off, she started to get amped some more. I was getting furious. I felt the evilness rise in me, and there went my peace. I got robbed out of it. The old me rose up and I failed the test.

It wasn't good at all to say a word but being saved you really get tried more often than not, and I'm not all the way there yet. My mouth is extremely smart, and I will let anybody have it. That area I haven't mastered yet. I love Jesus, but I'm in no position to let anyone talk to me any kind of way. I haven't gotten to the turn the other cheek, yet. I'm still a work in progress.

I knew then my time was near to be officially off this job. I finished the rest of the day, and I said silently to myself, I would let the owner know that tomorrow will be my last day working at the center. I got home and Zed texting telling me he was outside. I said well since you here you can come on in. We sat down talking about life issues and how to be great and do better even while going through. The subject started to get real deep, and then he said, "I want to marry you, Skyye on my birthday."

I didn't know if I should be flattered or scared. He said, "I'm very serious about you, and I'm falling for you. I think I may love you. I'm not sure."

"I think I feel the same about you as well, Zed. I don't know. When it comes to you, my emotions are all over the place. Marriage is serious. Are you sure you are ready."

He said, "Yes, baby," and started kissing on me.

I knew then he wasn't ready for marriage because he insists on getting in my panties first, but who am I kidding, I wanted him to know I didn't need what he had to offer, but the temptation was on the rise, and I was slowly yielding. Before I knew it, we had sexual encounters. He introduced me to some stuff I never experienced before. We got in too deep. God distracted me, reminding me of the dream that was now reality. I said Zed, we got to stop. I can't keep going. The more I told him to stop, the more my body exploded for what he had to offer. And then he released in me. Dude, what did you do? Why would you do that! Omg Zed just get out I can't keep playing rushing roulette with these sins, he left! And he was leaving out the door I screamed as tears roll down my face I hope to never hear from you again. He said you don't mean that! I'll call you when you cool down.

I'm just disgusted with myself. God, I don't know why I keep disappointing you. Every time I get on the right track, I fall harder. Zed text me saying he was sorry, and he loved me enough to respect that God comes first and to leave me alone. I ignored the message weeping to God because I'm tired of these distractions I have to get rid of. If I don't, they are going to have me in hell, and I'm in a place where I'm not about to gamble my life for Christ to feel wanted and needed. I'm tired of going through the episode of settling because I want and need to fill this void of loneliness. It has always been my heart's desire to be married, but somehow the enemy always gets me to a point where I have no other option but to yield into his status of tactics.

Often, I wonder if I really have God's love because I'm constantly going into the same cycle of longing for love; I give out but never receive it. This is the truth of what I am facing; insecurities and lacking so much cause me to be bound and love the wrong people and accepting the wrong things. God told me to start writing more on my 2nd book called *"Gaining Intimacy with God,"* and it's a poem that I wrote had me in tears. He allowed me to write that poem while I was hurting, in sin, coming out of addictions and gaining intimacy with him:

A Soul's Pain
Time heals all wounds,
With change comes growth.
With growth, comes obedience.
With obedience, comes purity
A Soul's Pain can be refreshed,
Renewed, revived, and become clean.
Trust me, you won't hurt forever.
God will wrap you in his arms
And never let go as you go
Through your transitioning,
Please know that he is there
Ready to love you,
Its ok cast your care.

Skyye Howze

A soul's pain can have one feeling depressed,
Lonely afraid, fearful
Not trusting God to work things out
Your mind becomes carnal,
Leaving spiritual behind, not knowing

That poem wrecked me. I cried myself to sleep then I begin to dream: *"I'm standing in a crowd of a whole lot of people and everyone is counting down to see the new person that's' about to stand before everyone. As the number got to one, Donald Trump appeared at the stand. Everyone was saying congratulations on your win to the country and I saw confetti and balloons released in the flag colors red, white and blue."*

Jabari bit me. He was my alarm clock. Lol. I got ready for work, made it there! I handed my supervisor the key, and she said, "Oh no, you are quitting? Why? You are such a good worker."

"I can't talk about it right now, but can you please call Mrs. McHover. I need to meet with her." She said, okay! She called, and she said she will be here at 12:00 noon. I continue on to work, and God insists that I release my dream to the public, so I got on Facebook to make a status and my God the backlash I got in my inbox was crazy! I got laughed at and talked about real bad for releasing that dream about Trump winning! I was scrolling through my comments just reading not responding I obeyed what God told me to do and I got off Facebook.

Jerimiah called saying he wanted to see me. I told him I would come by the store on my lunch break, but when that time came, the owner of the center was pulling up!! She got in, and she said to come to the office when you finish taking the babies to the restroom. I let her know with no hesitation that I had to quit because of a family matter. I begin to talk with her in private. The 30th day of October was the last day of my being there. She said she would miss how I did things around the center. Everything was always decent and in order, also wishing me the best in life. But I always felt vexed in my spirit when I was at work. Not only because of the spirits but I was taken advantage of. No one would go the extra mile but me. I didn't have a problem with working my job and others' too. Many thought they were getting over. The whole time I was getting prepared for who God called me to be and not being stuck in a position to work for others but to work for myself someday.

"Venting for Grace" God *as you prepare me (Us), we are ready for the growth and the fears we must face. We are willing to be used by you. Grace was there the whole time in the processing of me losing my way. I vow to walk with your grace every day, taking the grace to use it. My heart is grateful for every tear I cried and every struggle it help to break my pride as 1 peter 5:10 says: "But the God of grace, who had called us unto his eternal glory by Christ Jesus, after* *that ye have suffered a while make you perfect, stablish, strengthen, settle you."*

My Crown has tilted in pain, sorrow, disappointments, failure, and straying away from God, as it falls from side to side trying to keep its balance, God is right there positioning it to be worn correctly.

Chapter Four

Longing for Love

After I finished my shift, I went by the store to see Jerimiah, we hugged, and he kissed me on my cheek. We talked; just enjoying one another, sitting, and taking funny pictures; having fun. Jaden called. I said to Jerimiah, "Baby daddy is calling."

We both start laughed. I answered the phone. Jaden questioned me, asking where I was. "Excuse you…. you are not my man."

"Don't play with me, Skyye. I'm at your house."

"But I didn't invite you so why are you there?"

"I came to spend time with my son."

"OH YEAH!!" I said, "I'll bring him too you," hanging up. I'm saying in my head I'm not letting another distraction in my home because I know what Jaden is capable of doing!

I picked Jabari up from daycare and took him to meet Jaden. Jaden opened my car door to help me out the car, whispering in my ear, "Let's pick up where we left off at, I still believe we can be something great."

I said, "No. I'm leaving all this alone because I know what you're after. You and your other baby mama are still together. You lied to me and ran to me when you two were on a break. I almost fell for it until I got the information from a source that you clearly didn't insist on sharing."

"It's not even like that, Skyye. Stop tripping so much."

"I'm not stupid Jaden."

"He pulled me closer to him saying, "Come here."

I pulled away.

"Stop rejecting me, I want you now."

My point was proven. I knew it was all about sex. It was never about Jabari. You used him to get closer to me. I got Jabari and left. He texted my phone, saying," B***H F**K YOU!"

I laughed so hard!! Texting back, "That was your motive, but the mission failed. Have a good day, sir.

I got home. Lying down, I just simply began talking to God. Sometimes I can be overwhelmed with my needs but there is always someone somewhere that's in worse shape than me, so I am coming to you because there is always something for which to be thankful for and I am thankful for you. God, my family, the few friends I have, our home, our health, and the food you provide on a daily, falling asleep, waking up to a new day, new miracles, and a new month. I randomly opened my bible. God gave me a word coming from Matthew 16:25, "For whosoever will save his life shall lose it: and whosoever will lose his life for my sake shall find it."

Sometimes we have to let go of what is hindering us. We will never get to where we're supposed to be if distractions keep guiding our lives. No matter how the temptation comes or how many times you wander off, God will always show us the way back to him and I'm living proof of that. God will surely help you find your way and you will be stronger and wiser because of it.

Now I'm a stay-at-home mom AGAIN!! And I don't know what to do with myself, but I suppose God had me moving around when he needed me to move around. After all, I was facing. It's time for me to be still in this season to hear from God more and to be more spiritually alert. I'm down to two distractions and I have to get rid of them because if I don't, I'll find myself participating with the Devil.

Although one is far away and one is near, I still might keep both around just to have someone to talk too when I grow bored. But then if I do that, I might become more in tune with my distraction feeding it as I will be feeding my insecurities and loneliness just to stay sane. However, I got to get finish with my book(s). I need these next few months to be in isolation. I can't afford to be distracted. It's very risky. At this point it's vital that I stay focused. One slip up, and then BOMB!! I'm off course.

Finally, I could have PEACE and enjoy the quiet time while the kids were at daycare. I was able to study the word more, I mean get lost in it, learning more of who I am in God. Blog more, send out my Daily Touches and write more. I used my time very wisely because I knew God was getting ready to uncover what he had hidden for so long. I had to bury myself in my assignments and keep my eyes on Jesus, so I won't lose my way. My timer went off for me to stop writing. I had to get dinner started for the kids plus we had bible study later. All honesty, I had it in my mind all day I wasn't going but I figured I'll press my way no matter how bad I wanted to stay at home. I couldn't. Not only that, God was tugging on my heart, so I knew I had to be at church. It was always dead, and I will feel completely lost. the worst thing you can do is be stranded and not know how to find your way out to survive. The feeling of being lost in church is scary. I always questioned if someone would rescue me or will I eventually find my way while being in pain as well as trying to find perfection in my imperfections.

I fed the kids, and we were off to church. We got there, and I was led to kneel down to pray, to bow my head on the pew, but before I could even open my mouth, I heard God clearly say to me *your season is almost up here.* Your being under construction is finished. I have shaped and molded you for the next level to come. What I will have you to do next is broadcast more than just for the four walls of the church, your greatness is awakening, and your Destiny is pending. Get ready for an outpouring of newness. All I can say is thank you, Jesus. I receive it all. I got up and sat on the pew, still soaking in what God had spoken to me.

The Choir got up to sing and the pastor called me up to join them. I didn't say anything. I obeyed and got up there. I felt so out of place that I stop singing in the middle of the song. Heck, I can't sing anyway; why does the pastor want me up here? I just stood there until they finished, not being rude, walking down because truthfully that's what I wanted to do. They finally finished and she brought the word. the Scripture was Isaiah 48: 6; 10-11, "Thou hast heard, see all this; and will not ye declare it? I have shewed thee new things from this time, even hidden things and thou didst not know them; Behold, I have refined thee, but not with silver; I have chosen thee in the furnace of affliction, for mine own sake, even for mine own sake, will I do it: for how should my name be polluted? And I will not give my glory unto another."

And although I didn't understand anything that was said from the pastor notes, that word was confirmation of what was spoken to me when I knelt to pray. Ok, my mind is blown for real now! And all I'm thinking now is what if I would have stayed home, I would have missed the word that was fit just for me! WOW, God is something else. The pastor said we are adding a new member to the choir then pointed to me. I was like I know good and well God didn't tell you that. This clearly got to be a joke!! That is not my calling. It dawned on me that the pastor was trying to keep me in something so I wouldn't leave, but after what God spoke, I knew my time was up.

I didn't accept the choir seat, so she assigned me to something else. I didn't back down. I just rolled with it. I didn't have a problem with the Sunday School Reports that had to be written out to be read every Sunday before service started. I laughed on my way out the door! That was crazy. SMH!

My phone goes off. I got in the car. It's Zed. I haven't heard from him since our slip up. He said I miss you and love you, Skyye. I sat there for 20 minutes with my emotions wading through my body, finally giving in saying, "I love you too, Zed!"

"I called…"

I said, "Hold up. I thought I told you to leave me alone."

"I can't. You're special, and you are a great person."

"Thank you. I'm just trying to be everything God wants me to be but if I keep tampering with these distractions. I will never get there." He didn't have too much to say. I began to grow more into how he operated with me. Seeing now that he's not the test, he's the devil's advocate.

God spoke, telling me to keep my ears and eyes open. He's going to test you again. Zed started talking about sex. He had so much to say about what he experienced with me. Zed in one ear pumping my flesh up, God in the other ear pumping my spirit up. God said switch the conversation. I started talking about God. Dead silence. Sometimes in life, we find ourselves "Venting for Love."

Love is the most overused word in the world. That's what people say when they want something or have the wrong motive to get what they need. Well, I never received love growing up. I had to learn to love God's way. But as it seems, I'm not on the right track. I'm yet and still learning. The Love I desperately need can't be found in Sex and again my body longs for pleasure that makes me feel alive while I'm dying inside. But in God's word, it shows me how to love without opening my legs. It shows me the Character of Christ and what Jesus did for me on the Cross. I hope to experience that love someday, but right now I'm in a place where my loneliness overrides love. It has me accepting sin when I'm supposed to be walking in purity.

It had gotten closer to the time to pay bills. They have started rolling in. I had enough saved just for that month along, not adding in all needs that were unmet. Then I sat there, tears began to roll down my cheeks. I felt the doubt rise in my mind, and I started questioning God. Asking why did I have to quit my job so soon. I have no idea when my next financial breakthrough will come plus, I didn't have anything put away for Christmas for my kids. Not that it's a factor, but just to see them smile makes my heart warm and happy. I started to cry even harder. What am I going to do God? Loud and clear he said, TRUST ME!

I'm hurting because it's so hard to trust God when everything around you is dry. I sat there praying with my eyes closed. My phone vibrates. It's CJ. She texted asking what we were doing for Christmas. I said more than likely nothing. My family really don't come together on holidays. She said, "Well, we are having something at Mama's house, and we got the kids and your gifts."

Now, I'm a wreck. I can't even stop crying! I couldn't even text back. I tried but I was so busy thanking God, I ended up texting her hours later. I always say, "LOVE KNOWS NO COLOR." My kids and I are blessed to have CJ. She is truly an angel and life without her will be pointless because God placed her in our lives.

I'm getting up to clean my face because I'm just still in awe of what just took place. The doorbell rings. I open the door and it's my stepdad; a guy my mom dated when I was little. The last time I saw him, I was 13 years old, and when I didn't have my real father he was there for a short period of time. For him to walk back in my life so so so many years later, I knew this was God.

He said, "Daughter, I been trying to find you for about three weeks now. I reached out to one of your family members. Now I'm here. I'm so happy to see you!" Isn't it amazing how someone hunts you down to bless you? He said, "Well, glad you are doing good. I won't keep you long Merry Christmas."

"It's not Christmas." We both started laughing. Then he put 200 dollars in my hand! My mind is blown, and my head is swimming. He hugged me and I closed the door screaming, THANK YOU JESUS!! I know that was you; there's no other like you. Thank you.

I couldn't contain myself. My praise was to show God I was more than thankful but so grateful for supplying our needs. God showed up in seconds. All you have to do is believe what you pray for and here's a scripture to stand on to make your faith go to the next level. 1 John 5:47 "But if ye believe not his writings, how shall ye believe my words?" It's something to mediate on, especially when you know you can't make ends meet. God is always there to make a way out of no way!

I laid down in the bed, got on You Tube to listen to one of Jhene Aiko songs and I ended up listening to "Stranger." Believe it or not, God spoke to me telling me to pay close attention to the lyrics. As I calm my body lying there, listening to the music soak my ears, and allowing it to agree with my mind and heart of what I was feeling at the present moment. I started to sing the lyrics:

> Similar ways, similar game.
> Starting to feel the similar pain.
> Are you sure we haven't met before?
> I know ya face, I know ya name
> But I don't know you?

Isn't that crazy? isn't that crazy?
I think we may be
In a different book
On a different page
You said you are different
But you're the same
Stranger.

I put the song on repeat, listening to it over and over but didn't take heed to the warning at all.

Zed texted, "What are you doing?"

"Oh Nothing! Just laying here listening to music."

He asked if he could come over to talk. I'm trying to decide but I'm bored and lonely so yeah why not! And here goes the destruction. It was 1:02 a.m. Zed rings the doorbell. I open the door and he said, "Are you ready to talk?"

I said, "Yes," and he begins kissing me. I'm in trouble now because he's trying to communicate physically, not verbally! "Zed, no. What are you doing? I'm not about to keep doing this with you." Every time I would try to reject what he was doing to me he goes after me harder. Whelp! I fell into temptation and we had sex all night. But it was so different this time. Both of our bodies were taking control of the LUST that was exploding as we wanted more and more of one another. That made me fall for Zed extremely hard! After hours and hours of sex, I didn't feel convicted. I didn't feel God at all. I already had been down this road before, so I know how this is about to turn out. He allowed me to go deeper in my relationship with Zed and you can bet

Skyye Howze

I paid for it. We are unequally yoked, and God is not pleased.

Zed left me at about 7. I tried to go to sleep but my phone kept ringing. It was Jerimiah. He wanted me to come over to his house, so he could cook for me. I told him I'd be over later. I glanced at the calendar, did a double look, and realized my cycle hadn't come on and the month would be going into the next month soon. My mind is all over the place now. Man, if I'm pregnant again, I'm going to lose my mind. I didn't get a pregnancy test or visit the doctor because I was scared that I could possibly be with child. I tried to push those thoughts in the back of my mind but the more I did it, I got emotional, so I just released the tears that I was holding hostage! Weeping, I sensed that I'm about to feel God wrath soon.

There comes a time in our lives when we actually see the worst version of self. The image is so vivid that we continue to paint the picture of being that person all our lives when God never created us to be that way. I would do anything to be comfortable without changing and for me failing at it was my biggest fear. But as you can see, I have failed God from doing my share of damage. I spent so much time running from truths of what he can do through me. When he presented it to me, it was only to set me free from my sins.

I finally made it to Jerimiah's house after a long night with Zed. I still made time for him. I loved to be under him. He gave me a massage that I needed so desperately. To my surprise, he didn't try anything with me. I take it, he respects the "church girl" when she wasn't even respecting herself. He always called me an angel but what he didn't know, the little angel he

104

was crazy about laid her cross down, longing for love through her hurt, lost, and shame; trying to repair her damage with pleasure of losing herself entirely for a man that wanted to prove to her he loved her by using her body for his needs.

Did you know? God allows some things to happen, so we are forced to run to him, but in this case the "church girl" was drifting away. I sat to talk to Jerimiah for two hours. I left to return home, and as I'm driving God speaks saying to me, *When are you going to learn that my love only makes you whole, not people.*

I humbled myself as I could feel my heart turn flips from the pain I'm causing God because I know he's as disappointed in me as I am in myself. But if I let go of what Zed is offering me, I'll be lonely in my emptiness. The joy of knowing that Zed frees me from dealing with a lot, only if it's temporary. He makes it fade away because of how he makes me feel. It makes me somewhat happy. As if things aren't bad enough, I find myself "Venting for Joy." All the time, I wanted happiness from people instead of God. I would seek joy from being in pain, being an addict, being rejected and being controlled by the words that are spoken but never any action. It gave me great joy to cope and be comfortable knowing that I'm numb and unable feel what's destroying me. While I'm alive I'm dying to find what is the cure to be happy and whole. But at what state do you say enough is enough. I'm tired of masking everything. I'm tired of the familiar, and I'm surely tired of pretending.

The joy you are seeking through pleasure will not last long. The turmoil will, though. Not only that, it will help kill you internally; weighing your spiritual man down while uplifting the physical! Change is overrated but at some point, we all need it to live how God wants us to live. I lost focus and the demon of distractions took over. I lost focus on my writing. I had no strength to write I was praying for it and God did not give it to me. I suffered in my sins in ways I never imagined and because I knew better things were so bad that it threw me all the way back. So, I said man, forget these books. I stopped blogging, stopped sending out daily touches. I knew what was going on with me. God turned his back on me, and his wrath was all over my life. I stopped going to church, basically going when I wanted to. I just checked out, and God whooped me raggedy. Everything that could possibly go wrong was happening to me. My heart turned colder than ice. The old Skyye has arisen she doesn't care about anything or anyone. She's bitter, always angry, always complaining, evil, revengeful, and doing things the way she wants them to be. God has left my life so what else for me to do. My whole life for Christ at this point has gone down the drain.

I started listening back to worldly music, dismissing gospel; started back watching pornography and my addiction to sex was crazier than before. Every time Zed said he wanted sex, I didn't mind giving him all of me because I knew if I couldn't get the love I longed for I could get bits of pieces of him to show me I was worth laying down with.

In my insecurities, I was the damaged goods to a stranger who always fuels the fire to keep my sins burning. I'm sure I will bust hell wide open. The ship has wrecked and wherever the river flows that's where I'll be. I have rerouted my path from righteousness. I have fallen back. Just when I was getting started to be guided by my help (God that is), I was left to drown in my sins. The route we take always hurt us. It never benefits us from the lack of wisdom and knowledge and sometimes it's just because we want to do what we want. We could be very well educated and still do wrong; going the opposite way. Instead of seeking the holy one for directions, we dive headfirst into anything that sounds and looks good, which always, in the end, damage us.

The holidays are my favorite. I'm always in good spirits, but I wasn't looking forward to it. My grandmother will always cloud my mind and I will suddenly fall into silent grief, instantly going into depression. I'm crying because I feel so alone. It was so easy to share what was great to me, but how do I share my emotions. When I'm vulnerable, I'm unspoken; afraid to open up since I don't know how to overcome and unsure how long the process will take. But one day, I will be able to manage the barriers.

I had to shake myself out of what I was feeling. I texted Zed asking him to come over. Well, he couldn't because he was out of town at a job conference. Every part of me wanted to believe what he was saying but I felt so uneasy. I didn't say anything. He texted me again after I didn't respond saying: **We will get together when I get back in town.** The whole time in the back of my mind, I'm thinking, *Yeah whatever Negro. You with another woman.* I didn't trip. I called Jerimiah over and this time I cooked for him; just returning the favor for his generosity and thoughtfulness. We sat and watched movies and just enjoying one another, laughing and talking.

Jerimiah kissed me. I'm like OH NO!! You got to go. He was trying to talk me into it saying, "Just one time, baby. I got protection."

I said, "No. I can't do this with you." He asked why? "I'm already giving my body to someone else."

"I didn't think it would ever come to this point with us, that's why I never mentioned it. I thought you were saving yourself for marriage. I mean you wear skirts going to a church. That represents sanctification, doesn't it?"

"Yes, it does but, being sanctified has nothing to do with wearing skirts. It's a religion and a rule at the church I attend, so I have to obey it. Although I wear skirts it never stopped me from raising them up."

He laughed, "Girl, you so bold! I never met a female as raw as you. You don't sugarcoat anything, and you get straight to the point."

Truth is the only main ground to stand firm on. It's the safety to keep you free, even when it hurt others. You have to make the final decision to live, and for me, I had to stop being the victim of wanting someone to rescue me all the time because even with my cape on, I couldn't rescue myself. It's time for me to stop hiding behind the mask of pain, guilt, being broken, being ashamed, being lost and confused. From that conversation alone it showed me what was worth saving about me and that was the joy of being pure and having the peace to live for God even when others were against what I believed in. It was time for me to get back to serving God and stop yielding to what was trying to kill me.

"Well I'm just going to back off," Jerimiah said. At some point, I'm going to want more than your conversation. You are already doing wrong. Let me save myself from the trouble of getting you more in trouble with God."

I said, "Thank you, I will always respect you for not allowing me to go deeper into my sins. You have helped me pull myself up."

I tried reaching out to Zed to end what we had and to let him know the status of my cycle, which I haven't seen yet. He didn't answer, God began to show me an open vision of him playing with his kids. I said God, he told me he was at the job conference, and God said no, he's deceiving you. I called his phone all that day, texting still no response. I was so pissed! He finally answered the phone. I am trying to stay calm as much as possible. "What's up, Zed. Are you ignoring me?"

"No, Skyye. I'm having a fun day with my kids."

"Kids?... You told me you were at a job conference in another town that clearly your children and the mother doesn't live in that area. Why are you lying to me?"

"I'm sorry, Skyye. Please don't be upset with me."

"IT'S OVER. I'm done with you, and oh yeah, I may be with child," hanging up the phone in his face.

He texted since I had sent his call to voicemail: **What do you mean with child? Yes, that's right. I haven't seen my cycle in a whole month.**

I don't have time for any more kids

Well, you should have thought about that when you were getting it.

Skyye, I'm sorry that I'm causing you so much damage. I can't fix the mess. There's no way I can repair the hurt I'm causing you.

That made me fall in love with Zed even harder knowing that he accepted everything that came with me. He was the only one left that wasn't reminding me of my brokenness. He covered them instead, and maybe I wasn't damaged goods after all. Just a piece of good to benefit him while being damaged along the way. Now I'm thinking I can be redeemed. Life is so different when you fall in love with being numb. I was in an ungodly relationship that was so unhealthy for me. The love Zed was giving was filled with pain, lust, and loneliness. If only I could embrace who I am, Zed wouldn't have to embrace the scars that I keep picking, making them sore, trying to find love that's only abusing my heart instead of purifying it. While being with Zed, I was still focusing on my pain.

God wanted me to see that I was looking in the wrong mirror, while Zed had the image massaging my flaws and mistakes. God, on the other hand, held my purpose in the direction he wanted to go as I was facing the mirror of fears and failure. God is showing me on the flipside that there is hope and joy. Perhaps, even in all that I face, I still long for the wrong love, and God is willing to look past everything because he sees the full picture of what true love really is. I'm adding all the burdens and now complaining about the weight as they knock me down. Lord, I need you.

I'm sitting here writing in my "prayer journal." *Dear God, I'm coming to you for a redo. I'm messed up, my heart is hurting I can't sleep, I can't eat, I'm tired of all these distractions, I repent to you asking of your forgiveness. I need you right now in this very moment to cover me in your blood, protect me from the locust that's trying to suck me dry of all you have for me; stealing my strength and causing turmoil to my spirit. Camp your angels around me. Whoever is not for me. show them up. I need my fire to be lit again and burning for you. I have to get to my assignments and stick with them as you gave them to me. In your son Jesus name. Amen.*

I just couldn't get the whisper out of my head. I'm tired of fighting to change. How could I present the "new" me when everything is so familiar. My life is going in a million circles. I'm in the middle but nothing isn't turning around. My life doesn't make an ounce of sense. Instead of going forward, I'm going backwards (well at least that's how it seems). I'm so out of my mind. And I'm constantly praying that it's just stress and I'm not with child. CJ interrupted my thoughts as my phone ring repeatedly. I picked up, "Hello!"

She said, "Hi, Skyye. How are you and my babies?"

I said with joy, "We are wonderful."

"Well, I was just calling to remind you guys about tomorrow evening around 5 to be ready for the Christmas Gathering."

Before hanging up, I said, "See you soon and of course we love you." I began to play the Word Connect game and as I scrambled to find a word. I connected the lines and GOD was one of the first words. I sat there as the word got bold and placed in its spot. God spoke saying: I need to get back in my spot with him. Through it all, I have discovered there's nothing too great for him. I have messed up badly. But he is above and over all things. Nothing surprises him. I can say with full confidence that my greatest need is with him and will be met by him, not man. I have come to realize that God offers so many chances. It is true for me and equally true for you.

When I answered my calling, it was a resounding, "Yes," and through that YES, he revealed to me that I needed to know him. The way he thinks, the way he acts and how he demonstrates his love. God's presence from moment to moment reminds me that he is on the throne of my life and I'm not. He loves me and cares for me. God is my life. As I'm growing closer to him, life is getting more exciting for me. If you're worried that you can't hear from God, let me encourage you. There were times when I didn't hear from him, but if you show God, especially make time to come before him confessing your sins and opening your heart, I assure you, God will speak to you in an unforgettable and unquestionable way. Continue on your way with God, you will be on the road to great blessings and spiritual rewards - namely a life full of God's peace, goodness, and mercy. Brokenness is God's requirement for maximum usefulness so don't take your dark moments lightly. They would last only for so long as it is necessary for God to accomplish his purpose in us all.

I had to go to the store to pick up some household items. I'm in the car driving and my mind is going faster than the miles I'm driving. I made it to the store, I got out the car, and a lady stopped me telling me to get back to God, She continued on to tell me what thus said the Lord: "Young lady, I see a bitterness grooved in your heart towards God. It's not too late to return back home. God knows the cry of your heart. Allow yourself to fully embark on your journey to righteousness. Don't keep back-tracking to who you used to be. Its postponing your purpose. Forgive yourself, God knows what you have done, but you keep judging yourself. Let it go."

Man, this lady was all in my business. I couldn't say anything; just shaking and crying my eyes out. I went to the store to get needs for my home and never enter the store. Instead, I got a prophecy that wrecked me. I checked my wallet and noticed I had left my money at home. I would say I drove to the store for nothing, but I didn't. Those words exposed everything I was facing at present. I got back home quickly; started back writing. I wrote until I feel asleep. I woke up getting into prayer to ask of more strength to finish my assignment. I had just a little more writing to go and I would be done with both book(s).

Now it is time to find a publisher. I got online starting to reach out to as many publishers as I could. These prices are ridiculous. Lord how will I get the money. God simply said *I'm your provider. Continue to obey. Your books will get published!* I worked extremely hard to get these book(s) completed and I would hate for my words to go to waste.

I called Seven. We talked and caught up on a lot of things, then I explained to her that I was in need of a publisher. She said, Skyye you must forget, Detective, write and published his own books."

I was like yeah, HE SURE DID!! I truly forgot. She said, "I'll talk to him and get back with you."

I put my phone down and my stomach begins to cramp so bad I went to use the bathroom and finally my menstrual cycle came on. WHEEWWW, that was a close one. I kept thanking God over and over for sparing me. I was in pain, but I was happy too. And although I will have to make the best of the day, I would whether be hurting than carrying another baby out of wedlock.

In a few more hours we will be celebrating Christmas. I cleaned myself up and got my kids and me prepared for the gathering. I texted Zed and I couldn't reach him. I got on Facebook telling him to call me. He didn't. He texted from a different number. I said, "Oh, you got your number changed?"

"No, I was using someone's phone."

I was like "Whatever - but any who my cycle just came on - no baby." Then this negro had the nerve to ask me if we could have sex again. I said, "Hell, no. Your time is up. God has seen me through this and showed me exactly who you are. Goodbye sir take care."

He was like, "Wait don't hang up." He started sweet talking me.

I started to feel what he was saying. I started to feel guilty for letting go but what am I holding on too. I said, "No Zed it's over for real this time." I blocked him, losing all communication.

Never feel guilty for cutting someone off; it doesn't matter how long the relationship is or how that person made you feel. If you have to pep-talk yourself to deal, it's time for them to go, and if they try to make you feel bad for cutting them off, get rid of them fast.

They will sweet talk you right back in sins, while at the same time taking you for granted. Riding your wave, leading you into the grave, killing everything in you to keep them alive.

I'm super excited about this gathering. My babies are in for a big surprise. We are riding, and I go into deep thoughts, thinking about how God continues to show me mercy. I'm young and he is not letting up on me. The more I try to run and hide in my sins, he calls me and calls me until I answer the call according to his will. We got to CJ's mama house. Everything was so beautiful. They even broke tradition. We had grilled hamburgers, homemade French fries with homemade bakery and sweets. Those people loved on us the whole entire time we were there. We sat around talking, laughing, had so much fun then we let the kids open their gifts. I was in tears; just overwhelmed by how God did it. I had no words; my stepdad called me saying he was going to come by the house to bring the kids some money. I let him know we weren't there. He said he will come by the next day. Ok, so now I can't hold the tears back. I stepped outside to cry; just telling God how awesome he is. They called my name. I had to hurry to get myself together. I got in to open my gifts. I had some valuable stuff that I still cherish on this day. This has truly been a beautiful day.

I got a message from Seven and she told me to give her a call, but I was so tired when we got home, I pressed my way in prayer. God instructed me to turn to Leviticus 20:7-8, "Sanctify yourselves therefore and be ye holy for I am the Lord your God; And ye shall keep my statutes, and do them: I am the Lord which sanctify you."

God said to me as I sit to mediate on the scripture: Walk back into purity again, keep yourself clean in every area of your life. The work that I will have you doing soon, you will need to be in a place of purification. I said okay, God, have your way.

Instead of sleeping, I begin to write more and more as God continued to download. This was some new stuff too. I had to get clean paper. I poured until God stopped speaking. I finished and I was on seven pieces of papers in less than an hour! I was like, wow. I called Seven and she said he would help get my book(s) published but I wasn't happy. I felt so burdened it was weird. She was like, "I know how you been trying to get your story out. This can be your big break!"

She gave me the time and date to come to Georgia for the photoshoot and the publishing of the book. I got off the phone praying about it, and then God gave me Ecclesiastes 3 with several of verses: "To everything there is a season; a time to plant, and a time to pluck what is planted; And a time to heal; A time to embrace; A time to gain; A time to lose; A time to keep silence; And a time to speak; A time to love; A time of war; And a time of peace." God said to me: You have encountered a lot in this season. When you write, it expresses more than what your mouth can say. Your mouth is closed, but your heart is open to pour bountifully, and the words that flow with power to heal, not just you, but others.

I went to sleep; I begin to dream:

I was sitting at the house with my aunt, and there were two guys and three girls in a red car. One of the girls said I like your wallet, can I see it? I said sure. I turned around talking then noticed I never got my wallet back. She was taking all my cards out and stole my change as well. I was able to snatch it back, then my dream flipped. We were at a clothing store and I saw the same people. They were so determined to steal from me. They followed me everywhere; running after me for my wallet. Then I ended up in a setting where I was in the house trying to clean because all the dishes were sitting everywhere. It was very nasty, and my cousin was beating on my door. But when I opened it, it was an ex standing there. He came in because someone called my phone for him. I hid my wallet under the kitchen sink, and those same five people ended up in my house snatching my keys trying to steal my car. But when the key chain broke, the keys fell straight in my hand. They all were mad and frustrated, so they left again.

I jumped up pouring in sweat as if I was wrestling with my dream. I get up to get the kids ready and myself. I'm not sure if I wanted to testify about my book(s). I really don't want to attend church. I want to stay at home. I drag and drag to the point where we are almost late, but I made it in the door on time. I feel nothing; the atmosphere is dry to me. This time I didn't force a praise out of me. I sat there. I wasn't excited. I wasn't moved. My spirit was all over the place. God told me to testify. I did, and not only did I talk about my book(s) but other things that I have overcome. As soon as I finished my testimony, the pastor says in front of everyone, "You don't need to put your books in the hands of the people in Georgia. Your material would be in the wrong state and wrong hands."

I didn't say anything. I just started laughing. Nor did I receive how she came off as very offensive. How do you determine what being a saint is all about when you're around religious Christians? It's like if someone doesn't offer to be as transparent as you, your truth doesn't matter, or you aren't right in their eyes. If we are to make it easier for others to see God, we must share our stories more diligently, being open and honest. I wanted to believe that there were other people in the pews like me but instead, I saw pretenders. While my flaws were spread, my heart was bleeding because I'm always the one getting embarrassed in front of many. Church service was over. She called me in her study, saying, "I just don't see your books going that far. We can get with the bishop and see what he can do with your material."

Not one time did she encourage me. I was discouraged the entire time she was talking because I'm starting to see flesh and not the spirit of God. I walked out, saying, "God bless you."

I got home and I cried and cried. I was so hurt. I was crushed. I texted CJ to vent to her and these were her exact words: **It's time for you to find you another church home.** That was more confirmation for me. I got up and got on the computer to send Detective my first book. He told me he would look over the material as soon as he could, but God was tugging on my heart to still look for more publishers. I didn't fight with it, I obeyed. I got on Facebook and one of my Facebook friends that's also a writer was online. She inspired me so much. She had posted a throwback Thursday photo of her books. As I scrolled to read more of her testimony, I saw Wrighstuf Consulting located in a very far area and because of that I hesitated to move forward because the company wasn't around here. I figured if I went through with this; how everything would play out. It's not that I didn't trust God, but I wanted to be cautious in case the first step didn't work out. I felt like I was running a marathon with no finish line in sight; running with no way out. I said that to say this, we try to run all kinds of circles around God, trying to figure out this, that, and the other; when he has our whole life in his hand. We too try to get ahead of him; making plans when they never line up with his will. The truth is, I wanted my story to be out without being judged. But letting people see that everything is for God's glory. Who am I kidding? I was pretty raw in my book. Some can't' handle the truth, and when they can't do that, they criticize your words. If I could have life my way, I would still be trying to do my plan that never equaled up to what all God has for me.

Listening to God is essential to walking with God. God acts on behalf of those who wait on him. Obedience always brings blessings. You have to know whatever you acquire outside of God's will, eventually will turn into ashes, and if necessary, God will move Heaven and Earth to show us it is his will. God makes his purpose clear in our lives. You may be the only gateway to God that the people remember. Keep your faith strong and your heart in purity. I was no longer passionate about pursuing my plans but getting about my father business. Well somewhere down the line, my promises from God was distorted and delayed causing me to replace his will with my plans, now I have run into a dead end.

Chapter *Five*

Detoured

While I made plans to get to Georgia, I'm not sure of the route to go. LORD, I NEED YOUR HELP! We will be going into a New Year soon. No New Year resolution, just wanting more of God and all that he has for me. I want so much out of life, but I'm constantly doing the wrong things. I want to do right by God, it's my heart's desire and if it costs me everything, then so be it. I got all that I needed written down so hopefully, it goes smoothly.

I picked up the bible randomly. I ended up in *Psalms 139:6, "All the days ordained for me were written in your book before one of them came to be."* God began to minister to me: **Daughter, I'm redirecting your life for a greater purpose. I know you sometimes wonder where I am taking you, but my hands are hidden over your life. Others may see your unformed body, but I see the full you. I'm covering you. You don't have to be scared; in this season, allow it all to fall as it may.**

Tears are running down my face. I begin to praise him for his voice because only his voice keeps me still. We don't know how God will use a circumstance of our life, but we can rest as we know him to direct our footsteps. Though his hand may seem hidden, he's never absent, but present, right there in your situation, ready to be presented through you.

I called Seven, and she told me we could be on our way that same day. I hung up from her to call my cousin. He said okay, let's ride out! Our stuff was packed a week earlier. He loved to travel. Me, on the other hand, NOT! But it was a need. I'm so hyped to visit Georgia, a much-needed break, and fresh wind. That place always did it for me, but unfortunately, I didn't go to let my hair down. I was going there to work for more networking to get my book published. I was finally finished, OMG! I'm free to release my testimony to the world, and I mean everything that kept me in bondage. I'm now DELIVERED, HEALED AND SET FREE from it all, and more importantly I'm able to sow my words into others to get them where I am.

We got on the road leaving out. The drive was six hours. Wheewwww. I don't know how I'm making it through this. Cuz and I laughed because he knew how I felt about riding; it's a bit much. I'm pondering about this trip. I've been gone from Georgia for three years, I'm not sure how I would feel revisiting, especially going to this place to work and not stay. We got on down the road. I'm getting so irritated from sitting so I start eating, got on the phone, doing anything to keep from going to sleep, but I couldn't fight the boredom any longer. I begin to dream: *"It was a crowd full of people in the club, and I was looking around trying to keep an eye on someone who came with me. I'm getting paranoid because I'm around all these people. I walked outside; a gun is pointed straight to my head. I'm still walking then I took off to running, and while running, I got six rounds of bullets through my body. I'm still running, and blood is flowing from my body, but I didn't die; the blood was leaking like water, but as I ran, I saw a big white shadow over me. I got out of breath, collapsing to the ground."*

I jumped because of the noise the kids were making from the backseat. I'm looking around so confused. My heart is beating like it's about to come out of my chest. I'm asking God in a silent voice what is going on? Soon as I said that my phone rung; it was my mom. She said, "Hey darling, I need you to come see me. I'm at the hospital."

"I can't, Ma. I'm on the road."

She said I had to come out here because someone put something in my drink at the club. "I was constantly throwing up blood. I believe it was poison in my drink."

I'm sitting there, don't know what to say, tears are rolling down my face, not only because this happened to my mom, but this was my dream. The revelation was so accurate that it became a reality. I'm shook up! These dreams are scaring the life out of me and the fact that I felt all that was happening, it was so surreal. This is a lot to take on! I don't know what God is growing me up to be, but I'm not ready for this calling. My mind is gone. Skyye are you okay? I snapped out of it, saying, "Yeah, Ma."

I got off the phone, instantly praying for my momma, and just thanking God for sparing her. My mind is still swimming, and this ride is draining me. I'm going into deep thought trying to understand what God is doing in my life. This is all new I'm in awe. I come out of the daze to see my cousin is really keeping up with the traffic, we have gotten so far from home miles and miles down the road getting closer and closer to our designated area. I saw transformer trucks (18 wheelers). I'm so terrified of those big ugly trucks. My cousin made the phobia no better. He got between them, I'm screaming, pumping air brakes, praying and all. Heart is racing!! God begin to speak: **As you are being transformed, you will help others be transformed. I'm transforming you so you can impact the nation through your writing.** I don't understand, God. He continues: **On you are on earth to rebuild lives, also help restore people back to Christ, nurturing them back to good health.** God does not require us to understand his will; just obey it. Even if it seems unreasonable to live life as a Christian, you must allow Jesus to live his life in and through us. We learn more in our valley experiences than our mountaintops.

Seven called, "Where are you guys at, what's the location?"

I answered, "We are getting closer." She said she had cooked for us. I absolutely love her cooking; the woman can throw down in the kitchen. I'm excited now. Besides God, and my kid's, food makes me extremely happy. She said she couldn't wait to see my luvvies. I was a little anxious too. I can hardly wait myself. We got off the phone, made a gas stop going to a local gas station, not knowing we were a few miles from Alabama until I looked up. The stretch of the drive was overwhelming. I begin to journal to keep my mind free. I can only express my thoughts through writing. It always feels good to release pain on paper, letting the words bleed, leaving stains of scars and wounds that's been hindering you all of your life. I just want to be totally healed from it all. One day I will reach that place, but in the meantime, I'll continue to seek God as he takes me through the process of how to heal in this particular season.

We passed a hotel, and the signed said "Reserve Your Room Today." God begins to speak. He said: **The seat you reserved for you is not for you, it's for other souls. One day you will win a lot of souls through writing to a ministry. Some will stay, some will go, but they will get a taste of the word before taking off. Continue to reserve - (R)eaching (E)ncouraging**

(S)aving (E)volving (V)aluing (and) (E)difying for the Body of Christ. Wow, is all I can utter from my mouth. It is truly amazing how God is downloading things and how he can speak through anything LITERALLY!! It is way beyond my thought capacity, whew.

We were still in Alabama. It has so many long roads. I'm saying to myself *will we ever get to Georgia.* The road is expanding more and more. Trusting God means looking beyond what you can't see or do to see what God sees. Adversity is a bondage to deepen your relationship with God. You can be assured of some amazing things ahead, not just about who God is, but about yourself too. PAY ATTENTION!! To the long roads in your life, you may be looking and don't see anything. He is available to help you find your way, through pavement that's never-ending. Seek him on this journey. Don't lose your way. Keep traveling until you find that chapter in your life that needs to be worked on.

We finally got over the bridge, ALMOST IN GEORGIA... I'm looking at all these billboards, and how they are so interesting, showing all the great things people do to keep the cities and communities alive. I felt so sick. I closed my eyes to just rest, hopefully, get a nap in as I felt it getting good - the sleep that is. My cousin shook me, saying we are in Georgia. I got so excited. A peace came over me. My heart was merry. I discovered for the 3rd time visiting this beautiful city that this is truly my happy place. I have so much life here. With a big smile, I called Seven saying, "We are here!"

She said, "I feel you smiling through the phone." We both laughed. I put the address in the GPS so we can get to Seven's house. Georgia is so beautiful and big. As we ride, I'm glazed at the city. The GPS beeps. It was a malfunction and she took us the wrong way, but when we got ready to merge, it was a big sign saying "DETOUR" following up with another sign saying: "DEAD END." We had the choice to keep going or start back over. Cuz said we would just take the longer route and keep going. So often in our lives, we dwell on the lost without remembering that God helps us find our way. He is there being our GPS to show us the location of our destiny. When the road is extremely dark, and dead ends occur, and the road is so long, we can barely see the end, do you trust him with your next step or merge to get to the quicker way? Where he's trying to take us is being set right before our eyes. it is the correct route to the destination but suddenly we detour; uncertain, distorted, fearful and afraid until we find ourselves coming to realize that where we are not where we belong. And because of that, we don't know where we are or how we will ever get to where we want to go until God get on the driver's side, taking us to the land of abundance.

We pulled up to the house, and all I could think about is how these people took me in as a complete stranger. Tears of joy began to form. If it wasn't for them, I wouldn't be in the place I am today to share my testimony of how God kept me when I was at my most brokenness. Seven opened the door screaming loud, hugging me. I said, "Okay, I smell food." We all laughed. I dropped my entire luggage on the floor going, straight to the kitchen, sitting in the same chair I set in three years ago when it was time for me to eat.

Detective walked through the door, talking smart as usual. I'm smiling and laughing to aggravate him more, getting up from the table to hug him, He said, "Are you ready to work?"

"Yes, that's why I'm here." I finished eating, sat and talk for a little while, reminiscing and reuniting. It felt so good. Well, things didn't go accordingly. I started to get relaxed. I always felt like I was home. Peace always met me at the door. I gave him the manuscript so he could look over it. He explained more about the self-publishing and about the contract that had to be signed. I said to myself, *I have to really pray about this.* I don't want to mess up God's will; slipping up and not hearing from God, or going off my own thinking. I need him to lead the way. He told me to write the books. I obeyed, so I just got to see his hands move even when I don't see anything adding up, basically trusting him just as he trusted me with the assignment.

Seven said, "You want some wine. I know you are with the Lord." We all laughed because I'm there, but not there, yet, if you understand! She gave me the biggest glass in the house. "Girl I'm not drinking all this." I took two sips, and God convicted me so badly, but I didn't let them in on how he was dealing with me. My stomach started to hurt in the worse way. It wasn't the wine, it was God. I can't drink any more. She said she would finish the rest.

Detective came downstairs, handing me the computer to look for all errors and grammar mistakes. I'm confused because this is what I will be paying him for. He said yes, that is true but just read over your material a little more. I said okay and got to working. He said we would do the photoshoot tomorrow. I was hyped about how things seemed as if they were falling in place. I stopped looking at the computer and prayed because of me feeling so uneasy in the spirit. God was really dealing with me, telling me not to go back in my old ways of what I did when I first errored moving to Georgia. I open the bible, and God took me too: *Isaiah 1:29-31, "For ye shall be as an oak whose leaf fadeth, and as a garden that hath no water. And the strong shall be as tow, and the maker of it as a spark and they shall both burn together, and hole shall quench them."* God begins to speak, saying, **My daughter, don't get caught up in what you see. You desire a lot from me. I chose you for this assignment. Be watchful. There would be a fire burning in you, and many would try**

to put it out. The more they throw, the more you will go up in flames. You will stand as the test would try to knock you down. Don't be fooled in this season. Keep your ears open. Be very wise for many are plotting on my plan I have for your life. I took a deep breath saying, "Okay, God, I hear you."

Detective came back in saying I would have to come back to Georgia in about a month to do the photoshoot and to take care of the other business because of his hectic work schedule. I said that's fine. I didn't sign the contract. I didn't get anything published. I might as well enjoy my last day here. We went to stores to get clothes, but we ended up going to the mall. Before we got in the car, a guy stopped me showing me his CDs. He did Gospel Rap, which was awesome, even shared a portion of his testimony. I didn't mind supporting because I love music. I purchased a CD, went into the mall and came out broke. That's how it normally goes. I had a good time, but I was getting sad because I did not want to return back home. We got back to the house, sat around, ate, talked, and had fun until I drifted off to sleep. I woke up and it was time for us to head out. We got all our belongings and the kids. This was a very bittersweet moment for me. Getting our hugs, kisses, and I love you, along with saying goodbye, out the way, which was the hard part for me. We got in the car; getting on the road about 5:30 A.M.

I'm trying my best to go back to sleep. I was so uncomfortable. I said forget it and sat up and looked out the window because traveling is not fun to me. I don't think I could get used to it, although the ride irritated me. I enjoyed the silence however as we rode down the highway; my mind is relaxed. As I think about the goodness of God, tears roll down my face. It blows me how God continues to bless me even when I'm not deserving of it. Now my mind is wading, going into a deeper worry, not knowing how this could go. I don't want to bother God any more about it. He gave the gift of writing, the vision, made it plain, and now I'm in the place where all I have do is trust him for the plan he has, knowing that he will pave the way so my words can get out to the world.

I got on Facebook. I had so many friend requests. I was scrolling down looking and because the ride was so draining, I took the time to look more through all my friend requests. My eyes got big when I saw the guy that I had purchased the CD from. It was actually scary that he sent me a friend request. Weeks ago, before going to Georgia, I had stopped at his name on FB. When I was getting ready to accept, my phone rang. It was my sister, Tasha. She saw how everything went. God began to speak to my spirit. I told her I would have to get off the phone. I have to seek God to see what he is trying to say. God gave me *Jerimiah 17:7, "Blessed is the man that trusted in the Lord and whose hope the Lord is."* Then God said: **Skyye, do you trust me?** Yes, I do. **Leave everything up to me. You obeyed, you answered when I called, you completed the task, you**

put me first and the rest would be added. I humbled myself very quickly because if I would continue to get in the way, I can screw it all up, and I mean very badly. I stepped back and let God be God because after all, he is still in control.

The sun was rising; it was so big pretty and bright. I'm pondering to myself, saying I hope I could be that big and bright someday. The sun faded, and so did my smile. The sky got really gloomy. Raindrops started to pour down with fury. Sometimes in life, things can be so sunny. All is going well, no complaints, no worries, no difficulties, then all of a sudden everything shifts going left, gloomy, and dark. The storm takes over, the rain pours continually, you don't know how or when it will dry up or get better, but you seek God to brighten up the situation. No matter how things change, God is always the same, today, yesterday and forevermore.

FINALLY, we made safe travels home. All I wanted to see was a bed. I was so sleepy I didn't unpack. I threw the luggage down and got in the bed with my kids. I woke up to the next morning, and man, I was beat from all that travel. I didn't even go into prayer. I clouded my mind with doubt about the books. I was so discouraged, I just didn't know which route to go. So, I got on the phone asking for advice from a few people that I thought were happy for me. Hoping to get encouraged but all I got was negativity, and even through that God showed me who was for me and who was not. So, you see it's not always easy to trust other eyes to see your dreams. The way you see them is when you are in your place of being rebuilt while you are under construction.

Everyone becomes the fixer of your dreams and goals. They tell you how to fit your dreams into their plan to make it beneficial for them. What it should look like or what they believe is more attainable to their liking rather than yours. The best thing for me at this point is to accept the directions of the path God set for me because the acceptance of others is slim to none. I should have just gone to God in prayer rather than risk the judgment and shut down from it. Sometimes it is easier to say someone envies you or they are just the enemy. That maybe the truth, but at some stage in your life, you must admit that you are afraid. How do you make yourself available to accept your walk with God, when you have yet to embrace yourself in your calling for God? When you see that others can't handle the truth chances are you will believe not only them but the world, mainly the pieces of you that one can handle because you are fearful that they can't handle the real you. All I could do is ask God for the strength and wisdom to handle whatever is waiting around the corner for me. I started playing the word game, and before I could even scramble the word, my eyes grasp that it was **REPENTANCE**. God said, **Daughter, you have to fall to your knees and cry out in repentance. You are becoming too impatient in this season, you have to get in your rightful place, you have to keep yourself pure for this journey. Walk with me, hold my hand, and let me guide you to where you need to be, and not where you want to be. Sometimes you are too anxious.** I talked back with God saying, Father, truth is, I wasn't desperate enough for you. I let what others say determine my future. I became that way because I was afraid of what came next. All that was ringing in my spirit never kept me from hearing God say, "Repentance."

So often, life gives us the chances to be happy on one end and completely afraid on the other end. Those are the struggles and demands that come with being blessed. Your new normal changes everything around you. The blessing itself added more sorrow than joy, so now I find myself "**Venting for Faith."** *We watch everything but Jesus. It is impossible to please God without faith. When we focus on our problems, we miss Jesus. When he comes into our days, our everyday prayer or just a simple whisper in our hearts, we should recognize him out of context, basically expecting him in unexpected places. For your faith is what surprises him, not the familiar of what you see on a day to day basis.*

I got into the word, and I was in the book of Psalms reading Chapter 23. God said, go to *Psalm 29:7-8, "The voice of the LORD divides the flames of fire; the voice of the LORD shakes the wilderness."* I fell back to sleep. I even tried to fight it, but God took me into slumber. I began to dream: *"I saw all different types of families of many races in one spot just gathered and grouped up everywhere. They were all out to get one another; cursing fussing, fighting, killing, drinking' sexing each other, and doing all kind of ungodly things. In each race, some died.*

There was one particular person that kept coming back. I was the only person seeing the shadow. Everyone was still doing his/her own thing. He was warning me to tell everyone GOD IS COMING! For his people. Tell them to love and forgive one another. I screamed as loud as I could over the nations of people.

They ignored what I said as they carried on sinning. He came back while they were in the act. God came, I vanished. He got me out of here before the destruction hit, as I was able to look down on the earth. I saw a big mass of fire. People were running from the fire trying to get to God. He turned his back on everyone that disobeyed him. They all suffered from the consequences. I woke up weeping, going straight into prayer.

God, said release this dream to the nation. I got on Facebook typing the status, hoping someone take heed to the prophetic dream.

I finally accepted the friend request of the guy I purchased the CD from that day. I then got a message in my messenger of a link of a song called. "Tested in My Faith." It was a WOW moment for me because of the fact that I could relate to everything that was rapped, lyrically. I asked him of his name. He told me, Roman. We shared our testimony with one another, then I got off FB. God took me to **2 *Chronicles 31:21* *"and in every work that he began in the service of the*** *house of God, in the law and in the commandment, to seek his God he did it with all his heart. So, he prospered."*

God said to me: Nothing you did or doing in church is in vain. I see all and know all, especially the hard work and labor you did amongst my people. Even outside the four walls and for them, but you still have to wait in line because when I pour, it won't be room to receive. I'm still getting you prepared to prosper in wealth, good health, your writing, and in your life. The seeds you planted are soon to flourish. Don't take it strange when you see how many would leave you and find themselves back to you because of what they see me doing in your life. Man, God is filling me up with all this word, and I have to take it all in. There are times when I wanted to throw in the towel, but how can I when God is constantly tugging on me with the word. This season has been so rough, but in the midst of it all, I have to REJOICE. ☺

We had church that night to bring in the new year. if I can be honest like I always have been, I didn't want to be in church. I was tired of the same ole thing, but when I felt like that, I made myself go because I knew it was a word for me in the house to carry me while I'm going through. We got to church, and I'm just like God, give me the strength to endure. He told me to pick up the bible again. Going into *Psalm 29,* I said, "God I been there already."

He said go to verses *11-12,* and it read: ***The Lord will give strength to His people; The Lord will bless his people with peace.*** Man, God had a word for everything that I was facing, and I had to stand on it. I closed the bible and service began. I'm just not into it. It was dead. I turned and saw a lady looking my way. She smiled at me. I'm not sure how long she was looking, but when she turned away, this gave me the chance to stare to see if I knew her. It came back to my memory. When I went to the store to get groceries, she spoke into my life. She got up, and she began to speak in people lives. I said OMG, she is a prophet and I was hoping she didn't come to me, but guess what, she did, LOL. She called me to the center of the floor.

I stood there, and she said: *As a girl in your teens, you were forced to struggle, survive, and make it without much help. The way life worked for you, you were pushed into maturity at a young age. You had to face what was eating you alive and mainly trying to kill you, but here you are, standing on today. You matured by loneliness but were supposed to be matured by wisdom and by care. It's a very powerful yearning in you for God. You are serious about your walk with God and the experience with your mom is over. Just simply let it go.*

God is getting ready to pull you out of those emotional snares; the snare of the enemy, the devils that romp with your future. The attack of the enemy on your purpose of living won't go as far as God allows it. The enemy's tactics are curved. God is protecting you even in your detours of life. The enemy is scared of how many souls you can reach. Your faith, your mind, is going to be restored whole and healed for real.

I'm frozen. I'm shaking because this lady was deep in my business again!! I just busted out in an utter of tongues that were a genuine place for me, and I had to bow to God to let him know I was available in that moment of prophecy. She hugged me and told me you are going to be happier than you've ever been.

The clock strikes 12. WE MADE IT. It's 2017. I came over making into a New Year and new season in my life. I figured God is about to do great things. I made it home, and I rebuilt my vision board. God was giving me wonderful ideas of titles to my writings. Each time he speaks or shows me something, I write the vision down and dream until it comes into reality. I turn on my phone data. Messenger pops up; it is Roman. He gave me his number, but I wasn't too quick to give him mine because I never really interact with anyone online, so we talked on Messenger until I was comfortable enough to share my number with him. We talked about everything, especially God.

The conversation was good. I stopped writing to him as I saw my Facebook Friend post something again about her books, and she was acknowledging a woman. I scroll to see her name. Her name was Toretha Wright.

Then it clicked. She is the owner of Wrightstuf. I said, "God, this got to be you." So, I sent a messenger message to my Facebook friend, and she sent me all the information and links.

She said, "Call this number, Sis. She can help you get your work out there."

"Thank you so much!" I replied back! So, I was curious to find out more about Roman. Being an investigator, I went on his page, and I discovered that he loves God and is talking with some sense! Maybe he's a man of God. I'm not sure, but I will find out soon. I ran up on something he had written a month ago, and it matched my prayer I had written in 2014.

As we got deeper in our conversations through messenger, we started to catch feelings for one another, so I ended up giving him my number. I took a picture of my prayer sending it to him and he was just as amazed as I was when we saw our words were just alike. But the devil can fix things up too, so I'm not sure if this is God; in due time I will see.

We continued to get to know each other. I was getting ready to call the number that was given to me to reach out to the consultant about my books, but a call was coming through. It was Detective telling me I needed to come down to complete everything. I wasn't excited, though. I had a lot of mix emotions waving through my body. everything was overwhelming. I'm still growing spiritually, so I don't know which is which, but I did feel a lot of stuff being attached to me. I had to pray the burdens of others off me before I got too drained. I needed to operate in God, fully!

Things were moving fast with Roman and I. We had gotten to the point where we were falling in love and everything seemed so perfect. Maybe this is the true love I've longed for and never got to it! I told him that I would be in Georgia soon to work more on publishing my book. He asked if I could squeeze him in my busy schedule. I said I would see, but overall he was excited and was looking forward to seeing me. I suffered and encountered a lot of bad things in previous relationships. He could possibly be my last relationship, not mentioning we have a lot in common. I pray that I'm making the right moves in the right season, but if not God will alert me in the spirit to warn me. I called my cousin letting him know about us going back to Georgia. He said, of course, let's ride! We got everything in preparation to visit Georgia but this time around I wasn't excited. I wasn't pumped. I felt uneased in my spirit, but if I get a chance to see Roman, hopefully that will give me a boost!

We got on the road that next day, but I didn't bring both kids this time; only my son, while my daughter stayed with her other family. During the whole ride ,all I did was read the word and pray because I wanted to be sure that I'm moving by God's spirit and not off my emotions. We MUST obey God and leave all consequences, decisions, and principles to him because we can mishandle the assignment. Not only that, God assumes full responsibility for our needs when we obey him with an open heart. The awareness of God's presence energizes us for his work. You truly reap what you sow, more than you sow, and later than what you already have sown. Disappointments are inevitable and discouragement is a choice. Which do you choose today?

However, to walk in the spirit is to obey the spirit and initial prompting to follow the Father's will. So where should you begin? In your calling, in your gift, in ministry, or in your assignment? You can discover some amazing things ahead, not just about who God is, but about yourself and how he uses you to help others with the assignment he has for you to flow in. Always pay attention to what he says and how he says it when he speaks. You don't want to miss him, and your spirit responds prematurely. If you have to note every moment when he takes action in your life, DO IT!! And on your behalf, because he does appear to refrain from being in touch, but God is available right now to help you find your way.

We made it to Georgia, got to Seven's house and got relaxed so I begin to tell her about Roman and of course, she drilled me. I facetime him so she can see him, she said, "Naw, playa. I need to see him in person." She was very good at reading people, so I let her take me to meet him. We had a date at the mall. I'm not big on materialistic things but he brought me a lot of nice things, we ate good food, we had a lovely time. We stopped to get gas and she let him pump. She said he seems cool but be watchful. When he got in the car, she gave him what God gave her. We dropped him off to his area and I got out to hug him. As we hugged, our spirits instantly connected.

What I felt from him, I never felt from any man I ever dated. It was something new and it was something fresh. He kissed me on the hand, then he grabbed both hands and began to pray for me. I was in awe because I really never had a man to pray for me. So maybe he's into me a little deeper than I expected.

We got back to the house to set up for the photoshoot for the book. Although I felt no peace, I proceeded anyway. We finished and the pictures were pretty. I loved them all but when I stared at the pictures, it seemed as if I was hiding a lot of things behind my smile. Things such as worrying, frustration, uneasiness, and anxiety. I saw all that in the spiritual realm. God spoke saying, I have better for you, but I did want you to see that I can make anything happen for you but do not sign the contract. I did what I was told to do! We headed back out of town that same day because of my cousin returning back to work that next morning. We were in the car trying to figure out which way to go but we decided to go the back way, dismissing the traffic.

My phone rings. It's Detective calling to tell me I forgot to sign the contract, stating I can sign it the next time I come to Georgia or he will send it by mail. I said okay and thank you for your time and help; ending the conversation. We got further on down the road. It was foggy out there. We couldn't see anything, but in the midst of driving through that fog, God spoke so clearly. He said:

You see how you are trying to find your way looking through the fog, and you see nothing but darkness; the headlights on the car are helping you get to where you need to be so you won't miss the road and/or crash. That's how it is with your assignment. Things are foggy and you see more disappointments and failures, but I'm the light to shine through the grey when you don't see your way. I am the way even in the fog. You will be able to see clearly,

I kid you not. When God finished speaking, all that fog went away. Not only that, he protected us going and coming. My cousin realized he had left his wallet. After searching for it before stopping to get something to drink, we discovered that he also had his driver's license and insurance card in his wallet, as well. God's hands were definitely in the midst and I was thankful that it was!

By this time, Roman and I had been together for three months. He facetimed me, showing me a box. I said, "What's in it?? He said I would see when he comes to see me. We made it home. I got in the house and got settled. God said call that number that was given to you. I finally called and a sudden peace came over me. We talked and I shared with her about what I wanted. she got my books and we went from there. I wrote Detective on Facebook asking him about the book and if he had gotten started on it. He said, no, and that I needed to write my story over. I was like wow! I said thank you, but I knew this wasn't going to go the way I expected it to go. I had another plan that I already put into action which is the route I would take. I left that alone and stuck with Wrightstuf Consulting.

She called me giving me the price, and I'm rarely shocked, especially after hearing those ridiculous prices before. "Favor isn't fair," but God most definitely worked in mine. Roman called me telling me he needed to go to an event in his hometown then he would be on his way to me he has a very big surprise. I'm anxious to see what the surprise is.

Now that my books are out of the way, I can focus more on finishing my bachelor's degree in social work. I called my advisor at Delta State and she informed me that registration begins in April, so I really didn't have long to ponder or to prepare. My mind needed to be made up and QUICKLY!! But I also needed finances. I want to work and go to school but I know I don't have the support to do either. Decisions,

Decisions, Decisions! I will just have to pray to God. I know he will never lead me astray, but point me right into the direction I need to be in.

Even when you move through life with clear direction and a sharp focus, you naturally take the material and transform it into something new that people can benefit from, use, and admire. Sometimes we find ourselves moving faster than God. The minute things don't go as planned, we cry to God not knowing it wasn't the time or it just wasn't in his will. Your challenge then comes when you lose sight of your purpose, now your creative ideas are scattered. It's truly my heart's desire to finish school. I always wanted to become a social worker. I'm starting to think this isn't a part of my calling but all I want to do is make a difference in the world; to be an advocate for someone, or to be a voice for people who can't speak or find their way in life. I want to be that HELP! To get people to what they are destined to be.

Roman called me and we stayed on the phone for hours talking, laughing, joking, just having a good time. Before I got off the phone, I prayed for him and encouraged him to let God use him as he ministers for his big day at the event. I hung up the phone, thought on how my life is turning out before going into a deep sleep.

At this point, I had completely stopped going to church and would just send my tithes (if that counted for anything). I found myself in a desert place in God, the one I always ran to, I stopped running and started falling; the one I cried to, I stopped and started going off the emotions of whatever I felt. Then I was getting so caught up in Roman. I totally dismissed God all together.

Roman facetimed, telling me he was headed my way. I was excited, but I'm nervous too! I really don't know what to expect so I stayed on facetime with him until he said I'm in your hometown. I went to meet him to guide him to my house. When I got to where he was, he said are you ready for the surprise. I said, I sure hope so! We made it to the house; sitting in the car before entering, I asked him what it was he had for me. He said you will see when we get in the house! We got in, he got settled and we were sitting on the couch talking and laughing and out of nowhere he asked, "Would you marry me?"

Tears began to fall. I said, "What is all this?"

He said, "I know everything has happened so fast, but I want to spend the rest of my life with you. You are everything I dreamed of in a woman; I don't want to miss the grand opportunity to show you how serious I am about you."

I'm in awe. I said YES! I was happy, I was at peace, my mind was sane, and I was comfortable, but more importantly, relieved. The next day came and we went to go get married at the courthouse. We got our marriage license, but we couldn't get married until that following week! I'm on cloud nine. Not only because I'm about to get married, but because he was doing everything right - from cooking, cleaning, helping with the kids, paying bills, praying with me and for me, reading the word, etc. I didn't have to ask him to do anything; he was willing and made himself available anytime I needed him to be! "Baby, are you okay?"

"Yeah, I'm fine. Just trying to gather my thoughts together."

"Do you want to talk about it?"

"No, I will just pray about it."

While Roman went out to promote and sale his CDs, I would use my time to write! I can't believe I will be married. I really hope I'm making the right move and right decision because this is a big step, a big commitment and a very big change. Roman got back home and I prepared dinner for us all. After we got finish eating, we studied the word and prayed together, keeping ourselves in God and trying to follow the guidelines of Christ to be and do better. I'm still growing in areas so it's a lot I don't know and have yet to understand, but hoping to be led by Roman as God gives him the wisdom and knowledge to help us both stay on the right path.

Deep breath (WHOOOO); the time has come for us to get married. Before entering the courthouse, a minster Roman knew prayed for us and encouraged us to stick together as one. I'm so nervous. To take the jitters away, we watched the Steve Harvey comedy show, "Don't Trip, He Ain't Done With Me Yet," and we laughed and laughed couldn't stop laughing; the comedy was hilarious. It was time to walk into the courthouse. When we got in there, we gave the lady at the front desk our marriage license, but three couples were ahead of us, so we had to wait. We sat on the bench and before long, we were arguing about something. I was pissed off, but he hurried up to apologize, so we forgave one another and left it alone.

Finally, they called us to the back. We stood before the judge and as he read the laws, finished up saying, "Repeat after me."

As he said the vows, tears began to fall down my face. I'm scared, but I'm happy too! After the vows were made, we said, "I DO," placing our rings on each other's fingers. WOW! I'M MARRIED NOW! It felt really good to know I don't have to use my body randomly anymore. I can give it to my husband freely! We enjoyed the rest of our evening with dinner and him buying me nice things. We had a lovely time. I had to take care of a few things, so I dropped him off at the house to get the kids just in case I didn't make it back in time.

I went to register for school. I met with my advisor, and she said, "You only got four classes left, Skyye. What are you going to do? You are so close. I encourage you to go ahead and finish. you only have a year left and if you decide to do summer school you would have less than a year."

I took in everything she said but I only had one problem; I have no funds, so if I did want to go forward with this, I have to move swiftly so things can flow accordingly. I got back to the house got Zion off the bus and I asked my husband to touch and agree with me about the funds for schools because I desperately want to finish. He simply told me to stop overthinking and just Trust that God will provide the way. I didn't say another word about it, I started filling out job applications because truthfully I didn't want my husband doing everything. I just believe in working together. I filled out seven applications; some by hand and some online. Each day I was calling and showing my face to all the places I had put an application. The last place I went to was Cato's Fashions. I walked in and told the manager my name. She said, "Yes, your name rings a bell. I was just looking at your application. Well since you are here, you can go ahead and take the assessment test." God was most definitely in the building! She proceeded to say, "Follow me to the back."

When I got back there, I went straight into prayer, took my time and let God do the rest. I finished with the test and the manager instructed me to go the front as she scanned the assessment through the scanner. She came back out smiling saying, YOU PASSED!! Come back for an interview in about three days at 1:30 P.M. I called my husband to tell him and to thank him for praying for me. He interrupted everything, telling me he had to go to Georgia; it was something dealing with his mom. He said he wouldn't be back until after the interview. I didn't say anything but okay.

God spoke to me saying: **Your tithing counts. While you have been away, your seeds that were being planted is in effect now. I'm going to bless you with the job and even while not attending, still be obedient in your giving,** and I did exactly that. You have to know you can never out-give God; when he says do it, obey and watch the many blessings he pours upon your life. In our times of giving, we don't understand what God is doing, but it is up to us to trust him with everything. He knows, and he will be the one to give us rest when we feel like giving up or when things aren't going our way. We can count on the Master to get us where he needs us to be because he is the one that makes it happen.

I went to the store to get a few items to cook. My advisor called, asking if I was still interested in finishing up my degree and if so, I had to start making payments. My tuition was right at $4,000. I tried finding funds. I had no help, but I was still looking. She had said, "Don't give up. You have come too far."

I was thinking the same thing. Man, I'm hungry for my degree that's why I keep pushing to get it (and I will get in Jesus name).

The days quickly passed by and it was the day of my interview. My husband facetimed me to pray with me. I got in the car and *Intentional* by Travis Greene came on the radio. That boosted my spirit to go get what God had for me, intentionally. I made it to Cato's, walking in 30 minutes before my interview. The manager went on to interview me, I answered the questions the best I knew how. She seemed intrigued by my answers and that I had written books. Afterwards, she said we are done I will be giving you a call in about a week or two, but God had already told me I had the job. Her calling me would only be more confirmation and another reason to praise God! I called my husband to let him know how thing went with the interview, and then he finally said something. "Why do you want to work. That's what I'm here for?"

"You don't have steady income. I mean, your CDs pay the bills, but there are other needs that are lacking in the home. (With my smart mouth) you should be trying to apply for a job as well to have steady income."

He insisted that he would keep selling his CDs; that was better for him! I left it along to keep down confusion because I know how ruthless my mouth can get, especially if you take me there. I hung up the phone from him crying out to God in thanksgiving, just letting him know he is doing wonderful in my life and I'm grateful and thankful for the blessings he has bestowed on my family and me.

Zion wanted some chips from the store, and I didn't feel like going but I went anyway. I saw the hiring manager. We spoke then she said, "Oh, you got the job. You start May 8."

I praised God right there in the store. I know the people were looking at me crazy, but I didn't care who was looking and who was talking. I owed God that praise. That was my confirmation.

After Roman left his mom, he had to go to an event that was last minute. It would be nice to travel with him, but I can't because I have to take care of my kids. Now, I'm thinking, what have I signed up for if he's going to be away from home like this all the time? It's going to be a problem, but I didn't speak on it, I just prayed for him and with him to show him even if I couldn't support him physically, he had my moral support.

I'm still looking around for funds for school. I even considered entering the writing contest to win scholarships so I can pay for college, but I became so weary and stressed out knowing I can't work and go to school. God didn't bless me with the job for no reason. He knew I needed finances, but it was for my home and not school, so work it will be.

Whatever you want or need from God in this hour or in life, period, fight all your battles on your knees and you will win every time. Peace with God is the fruit of oneness' with him. he will give you that same peace in which everything you battle with. We have to stand tall on our knees and be our strongest when troubles try to come against the will of God. Prayer is life's greatest timesaver. Whatever you hold tightly to, and you find yourself slipping away from it, you will lose because it's not built on the foundation of Christ. Our intimacy with God is the priority that we need to focus on. It determines the critical impact on our life and others.

My husband returned home. I missed him all them days he was gone. We got on the subject about having a baby and I'm like I don't want any more kids because of my near-death experience after my second child. I was explaining to him that we didn't have to be in a rush. We had plenty of time to work on another child but right now isn't the time because we can't afford it. He picked up his bible, giving me a scripture. I'm sitting listening and I was like yeah you right my body is not my own so what other choice do I have but to make the sacrifice. So, from that day, we got busy making this baby. Whatever we had to do, we did it to get this baby here.

It was Day 1 of my new job and the manager showed us around the store, going over the handbook with us and helping us learn the register, all in one day. I'm a very hands-on person. You can show me something one time and I got it! She was impressed by how I was keeping up with her. She said, "Now the next day, you're going to be working this register by yourself. This is the only training day."

My body was so tired. I was drained when I got home. My husband had cooked, and he massaged my feet and back; he was really taking care of me. I was very appreciative for it. I went to sleep, waking back up to my kids. He had picked them for me. I felt so refreshed, renewed, and revived. My mind fell on my grandmother and I begin to weep. it has been three years since she passed away and I'm still grieving. It's time to end my grieving sessions. It's a picture we took my senior year of high school that I hid from myself because I wasn't ready to face the reality of her death. So, I got in the room to myself. Pulling the picture out, I cried every tear I could cry. I talked to the picture; whatever made me free, I did it! In this moment I found myself **"Venting for Strength."** I *couldn't find my way but all I know is I needed to be healed totally from grieving continuously. I'm offering up my guilt, my shame and the losses I took, giving it all to God. The more I cried, the more I was over the grieving process. As a child of a sovereign God, we are never victims of our circumstances. I had the eager anticipation that my strength was in my freedom, and* *whatever I needed to do to get to it quickly, I hurried to it because at this point, I needed strength more and more as I face life obstacles.*

On Day 2 of my new job, I got to work the floor, accessorizing the jewelry, clothing, and shoes, and the best part of my job that I loved, smiling and greeting the customers - my absolute favorite, especially assisting the customers find what they need and more importantly making sure they are satisfied. I started to feel lightheaded, so I went on break. After I felt myself getting dizzy, I called my husband to come get me so he can try to get me something to eat or get me something for the headache that was sneaking up on me. He said, "Baby you might be pregnant."

We went to the store to get a pregnancy test, took the test, and it came back negative. I guess maybe it's from me working; it had been a while and my body had to get back used to it! He still insisted that I get something to make the headache go away! He got me some aspirin, I took it. I got back to work and before I can even clock in, I was running to the restroom to throw up, but after words I felt so much better! I got back to work, getting ready to check a customer out and this elder lady said, "Sweetheart, are you expecting twins!"

WHAT.... "No ma'am, I am not pregnant!"

She said, "Your stomach looks much formed, maybe a month or two! Are you sure?"

"I'm not sure." We both laughed!

It was time for me to head home. My husband was outside waiting for me. I told him what the lady said. He smiled saying I need to receive that. I rolled my eyes. We got home and I took a long bath. it was an exhausting day for me. I tried to sleep, and I couldn't. God spoke telling me it's time to start looking for a new church home! Okay, Lord! I told my husband what God told me, but I ended up working that Sunday and we didn't get a chance to go to church. He did promise me that he would read the word with me and pray with me until we officially decided on a church home. I agreed!

My body is starting to feel abnormal. I asked my husband to get me another pregnancy test, and it came out negative. AGAIN! I had a doctor's appointment the next day anyway, so I didn't say much; right now, I'm just out of my mind. In this phase of my life, I didn't want another baby. I'm struggling with the two I have. I fell more into depression so heavy to the point where I cried myself to sleep and slept until the next morning. My husband woke me up to get the kids ready! I'm looking around confused. I didn't realize I slept that long. I felt so sluggish my mind was not in my brain. I was going through another episode of depression and having suicidal tendencies. With these thoughts, I committed suicide spiritually, dying to everything of God. Not relying on his word, but going by what I saw, made life so much harder for me.

After getting the kids out the door, I headed straight to my doctor's appointment. The doctor checked me and came back in the room saying, "Congratulations, you're pregnant."

I sunk deeper into my depression. I just found out I'm six weeks pregnant. I don't have the time or energy for another child. *We just got married; this is too soon. I just started my new job, was hoping to be back in school. I can't do this, Roman. I'm having an abortion.* I'm constantly ranting, *dude you have messed up my life. I'm tired of putting my dreams and goals on hold making sacrifices for others.*

"Skyye, I'm your husband. There's nothing wrong with making a sacrifice."

"It does when you can't afford another child!"

"well, you can finish school later. You have plenty of time; why is that so important?"

Wow is all I could say. He got angry and started talking crazy instead of this being a joyous moment for the both of us. I knew from how he was speaking things were getting ready to turn for the worse, and I would be doing everything on my own with baby #3. I cried so hard because I never saw my husband act that way. He snapped back, apologizing, saying he didn't mean to carry on in such behavior. We prayed together because truthfully I needed God's help. I'm not one who believes in abortions, but the thoughts were ringing loud and even in the midst of my thoughts I heard God say NO! Just as you have purpose so does this child. My thought was so deadly. I was coming up with all kind of ways to kill this child and myself. I really needed to be in someone's church getting a total deliverance before I'm in a grave.

The devil wants you to abort or cancel anything that God has for you. We can get so caught up in what we see and how we feel then before we know it, we have committed a selfish act to destroy God's will, all while we have been bent, twisted and furious by life. It causes our perspective to change and our future is distorted. Failure becomes the master while winning is the slave. Leaving God out, trying to go off of our own plans and suffering from the complete disaster for the rest of our lives.

I was getting myself ready for work the next day and all I could think about is how will I work and carry this child. My biggest fear is going into premature labor while working. It was bad enough, I was having those premature stages in my life, but I have no other choice but to trust God wholeheartedly with my marriage, the job, and the pregnancy. I have to cherish every moment, good and bad. I have to handle it with such maturity and discipline; I'm just not there yet!

The next morning, I went to work and shared the news with my manager. She said you don't seem to happy about this baby. I responded I'm not but hopefully I will come around. This is my husband's first child so he's SUPER EXCITED!

I worked on my assigned duties trying to reach the goal for that day. I went into a gazed as I started to open the box. before cutting it open, the label said: WARNING!! Wait and be careful before you tear open. God speaks telling me, **there are times in your life, daughter, where you are in such a rush and you find yourself in a place you don't need to be. You aren't careful with what I'm handing to you. When you tear things open, it's no good and it doesn't work properly because of the atmosphere of how you speak over it and how you handle it in that particular season. Even as you carry this child, you are in your birth season with your assignment as well. Whatever you want from me requires that you wait on what I promised to give you.**

I'm sitting here just stuck and confused and feeling like my head is about to pop. Jesus, what was that all about? I shook myself out of it because customers flowed in rapidly. I had to humble and pace myself for that busy day. I looked on that schedule and discovered that I had to work again on a Sunday and I'm like God how will I ever find a church home. God simply said, **Do you trust me?** I said yes. He said **you want to be on this job long. It's temporary and a part of your birthing season of how I'm trying to grow you up for what's in preparation for you. Just follow my lead**.

I heard some customers enter the store. "Good morning and welcome to Cato's."

They began talking about an experience they had at a church, so I moved a little closer to hear the conversation. They talked about how wonderful the atmosphere was and they were excited. I thought to myself, I want that, I need that. I assisted them with what they needed and while doing so I was led to ask what church they attended. One said, HOP-FAP. As soon as I was about to ask what HOP-FAP means, it was time for me to switch out shifts. So now I'm thinking from the time I got in the car until I made it home because I want to visit this church. I'm in a place where I need to have a church home. I'm thirsty and hungry for more of God. My well has run dry. I need my buckets to be filled immediately. I told my husband that he could keep the car this Sunday coming up so he can find us a church home because I had to work. He didn't like the idea, but I had to do what needed to be done.

The CD business was taking a downturn and Roman wasn't bringing in as much money as he was at first, so I had to work. I'm praying and hoping God blesses him with something steady so I can sit down. The mood swings kick in. Hormonal changes and my attitude is a mess, and everything is irritating me. I acted out and my husband just stared at me, and because I wasn't in a place to open up to him, I would shut down, crying uncontrollably. Anything he did to help, I wasn't satisfied. I'm sure he felt low, but he just didn't know I was feeling even lower. Life was caving in on me and honestly, I wasn't focused on my marriage. I mean, how could I be with all the mess that was going on in my life. I had to balance out staying healthy for myself so this child can come out healthy and whole. After I came out of my emotional phase, I apologized because it was never my intentions and I knew I was wrong. I felt bad myself.

I got a called in to see the doctor and I'm nervous because it can be some bad news. My husband and I went in and the doctor said I had to start getting shots from 20 weeks to the end of my pregnancy to keep the baby in, if not the baby would come early like the second baby. I was considered a high risk and could not be under any stress. The least of a trigger could raise my blood pressure through the roof. I'm holding the tears back. Lord, how in the world I'm getting through this? I'm trying to keep from going into a panic attack since I suffered from anxiety too. My pregnancy was a bigger issue than I thought. I didn't say too much to my husband and I cried half of the day.

Life is draining all my energy. This pregnancy is stealing all my joy. I have no desire to be compassionate with my spouse. I don't have time for my kids because I'm always tired and working! All I could do was take care of them. I'm simply losing my way. I started noticing how my husband was operating around the house. It was another burden added to the heavy load that was wearing me down. The true colors were in full affect each day as I observed and study his actions; he started switching up on me slowly. I never said a word. I'm just paying attention to the signs.

God spoke to me telling me to help him feel out job applications. We did five of them (he didn't want to) so we argued about that. I'm screaming and fussing, knowing I don't need to be doing that, but help is needed; I don't have time for slack. We filled all the applications out online. That same day, we went to Captain D's to eat and God spoke again telling me to tell my husband to ask if they were hiring. My husband asked and the same day he got an interview, was hired and started work the next day. I was excited for him; he didn't seem to happy, but the money was needed. Now we both have been blessed with jobs how amazing is our God. God is always on time.

I can feel my marriage crashing. Things were getting out of hand. I confused love and respect; I had no way of knowing the difference because I never had it. I was blind. I never knew love came with respect. I got neither growing up so in this case, it caused me to settle for whatever.

Roman got to the point where he would verbally abuse me' saying the most distasteful and belittling words to me. He made feel so low, that I rarely looked in a mirror. All I could think about is how does this man love me and has no respect for me? I didn't understand everything he said to me. I swallowed and digested every word, using it against him. But in the bedroom - he wants to talk down on me, well let me close the kitchen (No Sex).

He made me feel worthless and I can only imagine what I would feel while he's enjoying the sexual encounter. I'm lying there reminded of all the ugly words that were spoken and deposited into my spirit. I'd lose all the pleasure of intimacy with him.

The day is over and I'm restless. I just wanted to sleep, he wanted sex. I would cry and reject him because of the mistreatment. I didn't feel like a wife, I felt like a typical woman that had no value and no purpose to live. I mean broken to be loved correctly. I didn't feel comfortable anymore and I felt alone in my marriage and pregnancy. My husband was drifting away from me while I was detaching myself from him mentally.

Even with someone we can still feel alone, but some company is better than none, right? But because we crave to feel alive and wanted, we deal with the chaos, getting numb to the pain and accepting that others see us that way too. We try to convince them that we are worth it while their words remind us over and over again that we aren't.

I'm so EMPTY, I could just Die! My heart is turning cold and now I'm thinking this man did a 360 on me. This is not the man I married! Nevertheless, he began his new job and our schedules worked out, but my pregnancy on the other hand, no.

Further in my months, the time has come for me to start getting my weekly shots. I absolutely hated needles, now my body has to get adjusted to this pain while I already have ongoing pain in my life! We both got off work heading straight to the doctor. Before getting my shots, we got to see the baby's growth span. Just to see how the baby was forming in all areas was breathtaking. I got my shot and he told me next month I would find out the gender. I'm still not happy about this baby. It's amazing how this baby is growing in my womb. I have yet to gain a bond and have not been attached. It was a big disconnection, mentally, emotionally, and spiritually.

We got home and Roman was Facetiming someone. When I came around the corner to go into the kitchen, he hurried to hang up, and these were my exact words, "let me find out," and I went on to sleep, dreaming:

I'm on Facebook checking my notifications and when I went to check my message I had a message request and the name looked unfamiliar, but I proceed to open it and it's a woman my husband has been talking to, and she started to send me things of what they were conversing about. I could barely put the words together because it was blurry, so I exit out of it and continue on to engage with social media.

I woke up and the first thing that came to mind is he must be cheating. I got into prayer and I said God, I know it is more to the dream this was just a glimpse please reveal more. I start playing the word game and the word I scrambled was **LIAR**. As I tuned in to hear God speak he told me **your husband is hiding A LOT of stuff from you, he has not been truthful, and he is going to deny everything so be watchful.**

I received a message in messenger from a woman. She wrote to me concerning my husband, I read what was sent and responded back! That was my dream. It became a reality just as God showed me. I called him and of course he lied saying she was his "BEST FRIEND."

"Well, if that the case why I don't know anything about her, and the way she was talking it sounds as if you two are in a relationship. Is she's your mistress?"

He got angry and hung up. All I could do is cry. I reach for my bible to get it off the edge of the couch. God said turn to *Matthew 5:27-28, "Ye have heard that it was said by them of old time, thou shalt not commit adultery: But I say unto you, that whosoever looked on a woman to lust after her hath committed adultery with her already in his heart."*

I cried even harder because God confirmed through his word I'm shattered and Forgiveness is the last thing on my mind I want revenge in the worst way, my wall of defense is up I wasn't defensive because of what took place I became that way because I was afraid

165

of what is coming next. He came home saying he had an event to attend but he canceled because he had to work. So, he says he will have to quit because He's missing out on a lot of stuff. QUIT are you crazy or simply lost your mind. I'm pregnant with your child plus we are a family as a whole! He left out again slamming the door to go cool off, I guess!

It was time for work. He dropped me off. I was not feeling work today. I'm lifeless and my oxygen for God needs to be filled. I'm dying slowly. I prayed for strength to get me through the rest of the day. I guess this was not my day or the enemy is trying his best to swipe me clean off the earth. All these attacks are ridiculous. The customers came in making things no better with the bad attitudes. I SAID THE BLOOD OF JESUS DEVIL, YOU BETTER GET BACK TODAY! A sudden peace came over me as the devil flees. Work went from rocky to smooth. I got home from work and my husband said, "Skyye, you are going to love the church I visit," and he hands me a piece of paper that I didn't pay attention to, just gazed at. He said, "What's wrong baby."

"I had a rough day." I began to cry and immediately went into depression.

He hugged me, and I just cried in his arms in the car! I pulled myself together as I notice my anxiety kicking in. We got home, I checked my email, and my consultant sent me the finished chapters she edited so I could to read over them., I smiled, just thanking God for the connection. I got off the computer, threw up, and laid down. My feet are swollen. I'm not feeling good at all. My husband wanted sex, but I'm not in the mood for it. "Just please leave me alone, Roman. I'm not interested." I had no desire to sleep with him. I drifted off to sleep and I woke up to him forcing his penis in me. I'm not sure how long he had been struggling to get it in because I was in a lot of pain; hurting extremely bad! I felt so helpless then I was reminded of how my body isn't my own while lying there taking it suffering. If I told, no one would believe me, so I kept all the abuse to myself. I was my own secret vault, burning the secrets in my heart, and placing a wall around it. I knew we were a long way from being okay. I tried to train myself to take the verbal abuse, cheating, and now the sexual abuse that was lingering in my marriage. I was settling for heartbreak because he had already destroyed me. Now I'm walking back in brokenness. The panic was not about his safety, but the next heartbreak that I would have to endure.

Error is what creates our life. If we knew what we would be going through, we wouldn't even allow ourselves to learn anything about life. Come to think of it, it really isn't an error, it's a test and a trial that can either strengthen you or break you, and I'm BROKEN!! My life was falling apart piece by piece. My brokenness had overtaken the joy I couldn't find any more. As time progressed, I found God was stretching me. Through my pregnancy, he is stripping the inner me so people can see the outer appearance of how he rebuilds me, I suppose.

Getting these weekly shots is draining me. Everything is a force and I'm not sure how I will feel when things shift back to normal. My work schedule is getting hectic. I'm working extra hours to have a decent check. My trust in Roman was fading, causing me to be cautious with my kids so I decided to find a sitter while I worked. I know he wouldn't have done anything to my kids but it's my responsibility to protect them at all times. My aunt referred me too someone she knew named Alina.

I called Roman's phone over and over. No answer. He showed up an hour before work and we got into an extreme fight. I'm asking for my keys constantly. He's being controlling and demanding. I'm tussling with him when I know I shouldn't have been. He reached at me like he was about to slam me to the floor. I jumped back, grabbing my phone, shaking, trying to call the police so he could go! "What the hell you are doing, Skyye? You trying to put me in jail?" He snatched the phone, hanging up the call.

I'm still wrestling with him. He pushed me to the wall, screaming all in my face, balling his hands up like he's about to hit me, and out of nowhere, he shook me so hard, I felt the baby's heartbeat stop! I'm gasping for air myself, "The baby isn't moving, Roman WHAT DID YOU DO?"

He stood there with tears in his eyes, "I'm sorry, Skyye." He helped me sit on the bed.

I calmed down and begin to pray over my stomach. The baby started kicking uncontrollably. I'm crying uncontrollably now because God performed a miracle right in my stomach. I had 20 minutes before getting to work so I just threw on a cute dress, headed out the door quickly, so I wouldn't be late! I looked in the rearview car mirror and my face was red and swollen from all the heavy crying. I walked into work and my manager asks if I was okay. I said yes, I'm fine, just been crying. She said yeah, I can tell. I was so messed up in my brain, from trying to take in what God did for me versus trying to keep my mind off of what my husband had done to me.

Now, I'm fearful of him. I would feel such a chill of fear iced around my heart that I would lose sleep trying to watch him so he wouldn't do anything harmful to me. If I can melt the fear maybe, I could survive this marriage, or if I could melt a little bit of anxiety when I'm worried about my pregnancy of whether this child would live or die. I know I can make it through with God's help. I simply reminded myself to pray and trust God with it all.

When something is broken, you are determined to fix it the best you know how, and for me, I wasn't ready to face these fears. I thought pretending would give my heart the pumps it needed but it only made me foolish to know exactly what was happening, and still stayed in to protect this person, even in his wrong doings.

I'm at work trying to keep it together. I'm messing up badly. I can't function. I'm faking smiles for my customers. I was falling into depression at work because I'm afraid for my life and I have to go back home, and he is showing me different versions of himself each day. It's something new. IT'S SCARY!! I asked my manager for the entire weekend off. I needed to sort things out in my home and in my thoughts. She told me to clock out! I wasted no time getting to my car to release the tears. I started the car and *Deeper* by Marvin Sapp came on the radio. I'm just wailing because the song is speaking directly to my spirit. Man, I need to be so deep in God until I lose my way of understanding to gain his understanding.

I arrived home and Roman had flowers lying on the counter with a heart necklace. I just looked at it and started doing my motherly duties, not saying anything to him. Total silence. To give myself a smile, I played with my kids. They always reassured me that life is still worth living. Yes, the suicidal thoughts were coming every two seconds, running rapidly in my head, but I was able to look at my kids and say 'no, my kids deserve to see me live.'

When I got in bed, I didn't fight with my husband; I let him do whatever to me. I laid there, crying numb to the pain, not enjoying what he's doing. He's the only one getting pleased. I'm on mute, praying to God silently, *Please help me God I really, really need you.* I cried myself to sleep.

Waking up, I didn't realize it was Sunday until I looked at the calendar. My body was in all kinds of pain, but I pressed my way and we went to the church that my husband visited the past Sunday. I walked through those doors and OMG! The atmosphere was indescribable. Every pain I had suddenly went away. I said, yes. This is it. This will be our new church home. I got in looking around and I see HOP-FAP. Then it clicked. The conversation I had at work came back to me! This is what I wanted to taste. The Glory of God was all up in that place! My eyes switched and I saw the motto for 2017: *"THE YEAR OF THE BUCKETS."*

I had been empty, took losses, my bucket(s) was dry, turned over and haven't been filled in a while. This is where I would be Refilling up on God. I can just feel it in my spirit. They started to sing, and I noticed one of my Facebook friends, Kaige, was in their ministry in music. Just to see her being so powerful in God in-person was amazing because she was always speaking a powerful word on Facebook! It was always my heart's desire to meet her. She always grabbed my attention. It was wonderful to see her do work for the kingdom. I enjoyed service from the beginning to the end. Now my family has joined *House of Prayer for All People International under the Leadership of Apostle Joseph L. Young.*

We got home and things seemed to be back in place and order was being directed in the home. BUT I still have not forgiven my husband for what he did. I'm holding everything in. I got up to use the bathroom and his phone goes off. The message popped up from his mom saying: **I don't trust your wife. You need to come back home with me. Use wisdom, son.** A curse word popped up in my head that almost slipped out my mouth. I'm getting ready to pick up the phone to tell her a piece of mind, but God said no. I begin to cry. He walked over to read the message and instantly started packing while on the phone with the people, telling them he quit now.

I'm 3 1/2 months pregnant left to raise 3 kids alone while he just up and abandon his family for his own selfish reasons. I gave selfless love to a selfish person and he emptied me out. I had nothing left. I couldn't feel anything, nor did I want to. He had hurt me over and over, and the aching became the NORM for me. He was all I had, and he had dropped me into crumbled pieces. then would lift me up. I'm becoming an addict to the lie. Every time he says he's sorry, I'm self-inflicting the pain because I refused to let go of the abuse. I trained my body to get used too. When I lie down at night, I couldn't find words for the silence in my insecurities. In *Proverbs 10:22,* it says, *"Blessing of the Lord, it maketh rich, and addeth no sorrow with it."*

My aunt was doing the lady's hair that prophesied in my life! So, to avoid hearing a prophecy, I said I would come back. My aunt said, "God said stay!"

DANG.

She said, "How are you?"

"I'm here!"

"Are you okay?"

"Yeah," with tears in my eyes.

"Are you sure?"

"I'm not sure."

She begins to speak into my life, giving me what God gave her: There's emotional sickness, trauma taking over your body causing frustration to your womb. The devil wants to take that child out. You have bumped into a curse that's been announced over your life, but the prayers of the righteousness are going to pull you from under it. The trap that is set for you, you are not safe where you are. You are in love with a liar who dreams. What God showed you were just getting you prepared. The visions and dreams are not going to stop coming. That's how God deals with you, showing you things and warning you of the destruction that's to come.

I'm choked up, falling all over the table crying. She continued on: Don't turn your heart away from God. It's going to cause you your sanity. God wants you to bare much fruit. You have a snake in your life **sent on assignment to rob you out of your calling to abort your purpose and plan**. I receive every word I'm in awe. It was at a turning point for me. I realized that through my identity, the emotions I had to learn wasn't enough about myself, I had to dig deeper. I couldn't just walk away on the verge of an emotional eruption. The maturity of staying in this marriage even after I got the prophecy will be required to help me grow up, to developing such a deep thirst for God and a stronger relationship.

I'm in between pressure and joy. I'm so POWERLESS in this big combustion of sorrow. My crown is extremely heavy, but I know I'm not in this alone and don't have to carry it on my own. I will take this chaos and walk with boldness, authority, wisdom, and discernment because at this point. My walk with Christ is leaning. I'm not there FULLY! My faith really needs to be restored through these thorns of hardship that's tearing me apart.

Chapter Six

Beautiful Chaos

I had a doctor's appointment coming up for the gender of the baby! My husband and I aren't talking, so I'm trying to decide if I want to call him or not. Well, I put my pride and emotions to the side, and he said he would try to make it since I had nothing else to say. I quickly hung up. I'm running off fumes, I'm weak, and I'm still pressing while being weary.

There are some things that love shouldn't allow you to do. What is the definition of Love? How would I know when I never received Love as a child! When your marriage seems as if it was a whole lie? I got so far from who I was as a person and in God, I felt in that moment that if I would revert back to the old version of me, maybe things will be for the best. All hell was breaking loose; something I didn't see coming. I'm in a place of questioning myself am I enough? What's the problem? Why did this man abandon us?

I got ready for work, got there, getting ready to clock in, and my manager said you aren't on the schedule for today! I came in on the wrong day, so I went to go get back in my car. My gas light comes on. I'm sitting there saying, Lord all I have is 10 dollars, and I need other stuff as well. The needs are great, God. I drove, and I saw a man holding up a sign saying in need of gas. God said, give the man the money. Why God? He said, do you trust me? I humbled myself and gave it to him with a smile while breaking inside. It was my last and knowing this was my last, I drove home on Empty! I got in the driveway. I was led to check my bank card on my phone. I had $250 on it! OMG! WOW! WHAT! WAIT! I had gone to work on a wrong day, but if I hadn't shown up, I would have missed out on the miraculous move of God!

A little wisdom from me to you. When he Speaks, Listen and Obey; you will forever be blessed! God will always take care of you. Trust him in whatever season you may be in. Depend on him solely because of the situation I was in, I most certainly did! I cried like a baby because I just couldn't grasp what had happened. Even though I had faith, God's awesomeness always overwhelms me.

Roman texted me this long ridiculous paragraph that I didn't care to read. I just don't see the reason for him texting me when he left me. It is something when you're married and still a single parent. I just want the pain to go away; it's unbearable. I get another message in my messenger. It's the woman Roman was talking to and she began to tell me more things about the two of them. I responded and this time it wasn't kind. I don't like drama, so I screenshot everything that was said, and when I confronted him, he lied again. I'm furious because he is protecting this woman more than he ever protected me. The lie added to another secret that was held back but revealed. It thickened the wall around my heart. How could he ever fully give pure love if he was struggling to love and accept me? But we were married so there wasn't much I could do about it. I had to sit and take a lot of stuff. I shouldn't be under any stress; I could lose my baby.

I was on my phone playing the word game to relieve some of my anxiety. I connected the dots and there is the word: **WOUND.** At the root of the problem, I wanted to be HEALED from the damage he caused me. I felt like all he wanted was a distraction from his pain. He would tear me down with his words allowing them to attack my brokenness. I learned quickly to suffer and pray without ceasing while I hoped the man I loved would learn to love himself so he can stop using me as a tool for abuse. I picked up my bible, turning to *Jerimiah 27:2 "Thus said the Lord to me: Make thee bonds and yokes and put them upon thy neck."*

I always had a major problem opening up, and I couldn't talk to my husband about anything because he would belittle me, bash me with the word of God, and judge me in the worst ways. The communication had been stifled in my heart. I knew he didn't love me much because he always lied; never protecting my heart. He would rather lie than tell the truth, and I continue on to accept all lies. It was love on his level even though it broke me and brought me down. At some point, I had to hide the lies as it slipped its way in my insecurities. I no longer felt like the prize because the "Best friend" was getting the attention I never received. I came to terms that I married a false image of what a man is supposed to be as a husband. All of this is a nightmare.

We attended church, but this time my husband was absent. While there I'm lost and have no understanding of what is going on in my life. But I worship God, nonetheless.

Service was awesome. After the Word went forward, I think the pastor called Altar Call or Prayer. I'm not sure, but I hesitated to go up. I stood five minutes, and Zion said, "Ma, you need to go up there."

Tears formed and I went up. I'm nervous, I'm shaking. Finally, he gets to me. My hands are wet with sweat. He said, "You have been in search of a place for a long time, you have been in a very dry place. Where you came from was very traditional and religious, and there's nothing there to challenge you in your walk with Christ. I also see books and businesses in you. God is going to do some supernatural things in your life."

I'm standing in a state of shock because now this man is all in my business. Especially about the books and businesses. I'm scared for real now! That blew me away, but it also gave me assurance that I was doing the right thing. I walk back to my seat, calm, mind clear because I have confirmation. Now that my books are in fulfillment and on the way, I'm sure whatever next he has for me is soon to come as well.

When service was over all that was in my spirit "PRESS IN MY PREGNANCY." As my stomach is getting bigger, I had to also be bigger in God, continue to come to church every time the doors opened. I knew my strength was in God's house, and I did press the whole nine months. So, when you don't feel like going, that's the time to go. When you press, God gives you an extra boost to get through it all. As you face this process, it shows others that the stretch can be made with a faithful heart and mind. Many times, people make excuses. In this season of my life, I couldn't afford to make any excuses. My help came from the Lord. Pregnant and all, every time the doors were open, I was there. I owed God my life, and whatever it takes, I have to press to get to my destiny.

It was time to visit the doctor to see what the sex was of the child we were having. Roman called telling me he was pulling up in town. We met one another at the doctor's office. I didn't have much to say but not to be rude, I spoke to him and we walked in the building together. As we entered, they were calling my name, so we went straight to the back. I proceeded with the normal routine, including the shot. Finishing up with that part, the lady rubbed cold jelly on my stomach. I'm staring at the screen, tears form because now I'm starting to feel excitement for this baby. My heart is burning with love. I'm ready to give my all to this child now, and once it enters into the world.

We have discovered that we are having a GIRL! Wow, another princess added to the family. We walked out the doctor's office and Roman begins to pour his heart out crying and we both are shedding tears. I'm vulnerable and emotional as it is! So, I'm feeding into everything he is saying. We made a decision right there that we would work things out. He said he would move back in after he handled some business and attend the two events that he had coming up for this month. We went to the park to sit and talk. He is saying to me, "I'm sorry for putting you through a lot. Blaming you. I can't use an excuse for my wrong doings. I'm imperfect and I know God can help me be who he called me to be. I repented to God for how I've treated you and I'm praying that God changes your heart towards me. You are beautiful, you are smart, and you are very funny."

We laughed!!

"You have a good heart. When I left, I thought about you all the time and I really missed you. I want you back in my life. Can we please make things right?"

Any little sign he showed me of becoming the kind of man I desired and dreamed of, it was easier for me to take him back with no hesitation, allowing myself to stay in a little longer. It wasn't a balanced thing but the hope he gave me with his words was enough to say I'm willing to fight for my marriage.

We got back to the house and he pampered me all that day. He was very attentive to me, but I wasn't happy. I was afraid and fearful, remembering all he had done to me. I tried to keep myself from breaking, but I couldn't hold the cry in any longer. I wailed and wailed trying to keep from going into a panic attack. My mind is all over the place, I'm confused, and don't know the outlook of this marriage. I'm flowing in emotions, so I picked up the bible, turning to *Psalm 25:17, "The troubles of my heart are enlarged o bring thou me out of distress."*

Lord help me to weigh all of this out. I'm pondering and it is causing me to **"Vent for Forgiveness."**

Life has always been a drag for me. I'm on the blindside trying to reach my faith but I'm drowning in my sorrow. I can't seem to see my way. My soul is yearning for tangible things that causes my body to leap for harm, hurt, danger, pain, and abuse that I don't need. Where is the way to healing, comfort, joy, security, and love? Somehow depression and anxiety alarm me to wake me up so I can continue on with my everyday episode of dying instead of living. I don't have the heart to forgive. I choose to keep it all in. Honestly, if I let go of what's keeping me numb, what do I have left to feed my soul.

The things he had to do were put off until a later time, so he never went back to Georgia. He stayed. He was out of a job so he sold CDs to help out with whatever he could. I'm really trying to be cautious. I'm walking on eggshells in my own home.

It was time for bed, so we prayed and read the word together. I need to replace this fear with faith, hoping things will come in alignment and we be as one. My spirit became vexed, thinking to myself, I feel like he is going to walk out on me again. I know I shouldn't think negative. I'm trying to look at the positive side of all of this, but my mind keeps triggering back to what he has done. My finances are just crazy. I have to pay Alina for watching my kids and also take care of my business with God (tithing that is). God gets the first fruit before I do anything with my money! I never have anything to myself because the bills eat all of what I have left. I'm struggling and in a very hard place. I'm trying not to stress. Everything is FALLING APART!

We went to church and the sermon for service was "Living by My Giving." At this point in my life, I have no other choice but to trust him with my finances, and I do that. Every paycheck I get, I tithed out of it, giving him his 10 percent, because I know if I continue on to be obedient in my giving, applying the principle to do as the word says, God is going to take care of me. Supplying all my needs, according to his riches and glory.

I'm giving my all from the seeds I'm sowing yet and still see NO RESULTS! I'm reaching, trying to gain everything he has for me but there's nothing there, but more problems and life is getting extremely harder. Roman and I were going to church every Sunday. We had so many problems to sort out. We tried to tackle each one as much as we could. We were only four months into our marriage when we both went to the pastor to see could we have counseling sessions. The first couple of sessions weren't easy.

We both had to take responsibility for the things we did, especially the hurt that spread. In this moment, I felt like God was honoring our commitment to at least try to be better for him and one another. But things were backtracking and backfiring on me from what he was doing, and in the midst of it, I felt my body shutting down from all the tension and stress.

I can't believe this man is acting like this. While I suffer, I feel my heart bruised but I allow him to finish damaging me without saying anything. I just ignored the pain that I was used to, turning over to go to sleep. I tried to create safety in my marriage but there is no fence to cover me. It even feels like God is not there, seeing now that I'm in DANGER. My fear is becoming bigger than my problems. I got ready for work and I get a video call from his "supposed to be Best Friend." I didn't answer, so she sent a message through messenger. I'm so tired of this girl because now she is 'picking.' I went off on her and the more upset she became, the more information she revealed. I wanted to leave it alone, but I pretended to keep going because I knew there was more. When I confronted Roman about her, he denied it once again. I'm calling, texting, sending screenshots, and lacing it with obscenities, then he finally responded. "She is just my best friend; someone I could talk to. Nothing more."

"YOU A LIAR! I have all the messages right here." Plus, the girl had a different story. When I asked him about that, he was still lying, trying to save face, saying, "She just mad because I didn't marry her. She caught feelings for me and trying to destroy what we have!"

I just put my phone down, now I'm stuck between the lies he told me and the lies he told her, but I know there is still pieces missing and I will find out. No matter how much you accept an insecure person, you can never make them love or accept themselves. I kept telling myself, if I showed Roman that he was still lovable, he would no longer need validation from other women. It was bigger than other women. This man was battling with a lusting spirit. In all areas of my life, the more I gave, the more he took from me. He left and told me, "This time I'm not coming back. Figure it out on your own."

I'm shattered, I'm a total wreck, I'm praying and crying out to God, asking him what I have done to deserve this type of treatment. I begin reading the bible looking for a certain scripture to gain comfort in the moment of going through. God took me to *Zechariah 2:5, "For I saith the Lord will be unto her a wall of fire about and will be their Glory in the midst of her."*

God spoke saying: *I am your HELP to come out of the fire. You have to be thrown in the fire. But while you're in it, I'm with you. This beautiful chaos isn't designed to destroy you. It's to build you. Don't take anything lightly. What is happening in your marriage, learn from it, grow in it, and walk it out. You remember when you asked me to FILL YOU UP? I'm doing so by stripping, shredding, and sweeping. My glory is on your life. Stand strong, enduring to the end. The more the fire blazes, I will be there to cool it down in every situation.*

I'm really thinking about quitting my job. This is too much to bare. While being pregnant, I have a lot on my plate. Things are being stacked on top of one another. There's no room to put my other burdens. All I could think about is how my husband came in this marriage with this lusting spirit (that he never mentioned). It also dawned on me, maybe he's dealing with something mentally and I really wanted to find out why he is abusive because it's affecting my life. The abuse was robbing me out of everything. My excitement for God has lessened. My freedom has turned into fear. My joy is ringing in pain, and my happiness in my marriage has died. Who am I? I'm crying, and I walk to the kitchen. Opening up the drawer, I pull out the biggest knife I could find. Standing there leaning my head back, sobbing and pressing in on my throat. As soon as I was about to press in harder, Zion called out, "Ma."

I hurried to put the knife behind my back. "Yes, Zion?"

"I love you, Ma!"

I broke right there in front of her. She was my interruption sent by God. I held on to her so tight because she always keeps me alive with her words, and she also saved her baby sister's life as well. When I released myself from her, she rubbed my stomach smiling, saying, "I can't wait to meet my little sister so I can put make up and lip gloss on her."

That was so funny, and it brightened my day. I thought it was the cutest.

I'm looking around to see what I'm lacking, and it's just about everything. All I had left from my check, after paying my tithes last Sunday and getting bills paid, was $4.50. Since I got paid every two weeks, I didn't have anything to put in church so all I had left I was going to sow it. We had service and the pastor made an announcement saying after we sow our general offering, we would do a second offering sowing a seed on behalf of someone who's in need. I'm sitting in church dividing my money, doing $2.50 for general offering and $2.00 to sow a seed.

Worship was going on and Kaige ministered to my broken soul through music singing, *I Want More of You God*. My eyes are glued on her the whole time and I just burst into tears, allowing God to show me that I couldn't make it in life without him. The time came and the pastor said, "Prepare your hearts to give cheerfully."

I'm digging in my wallet when the pastor said, "Skyye come up to the altar."

My eyes got big. I said silently, WHAT! Tears are forming. He handed me the bucket, instructing me to turn to the front as the members came up sowing there seeds. God spoke right there saying, I told you I was going to take care of you. I was so emotional. I hugged my pastor and just thanking him and Thanking God that turned my whole world upside down. I came to church with $4.50, leaving out with $729.00. Before I even left the parking lot, I tithed out the seed that was sowed in my life, giving God his 10 percent back, plus the money I took out so now I have money to plant for next Sunday.

If this wasn't enough to blow my mind, I got home and had a box of household supplies sitting by my door. I don't even know what to do with myself. Not only that, Alina knocked on my door with bags of groceries. Now I'm swimming in the head. When God pours, he POURS bountifully in my life! Just when I thought he forgot about me, he came in the midst of my deficit, showing me that his hand was the provider when my eyes didn't see how he would make ends meet.

Time is getting closer. I'm now 6 and 1/2 months pregnant and it's been almost 7 and 1/2 months on my job. I'm having a lot of complications with my pregnancy at work. My back and feet are always hurting and swollen. My vision is bad, my ears ache each day, and these shots are getting on my nerves!

I'm cooking and cleaning. I felt a sharp pain, but I ignored it. The pain came back stronger. I said, OH NO, I hope this little girl isn't trying to come. Looking down, I see spots of blood on my pants. I called Alina after I couldn't reach anyone else, to take me to the doctor. She got me to doctor and also helped me with my kids.

The doctor checked me saying, she wasn't trying to come, but it could possibly happen because of the stress that was taking over my body. He sends me to the hospital so I could be put on a fetal monitor for an hour, but instead, I was admitted. I called Roman. He was too busy worrying about himself, he rushed me off the phone. The nurse rolled me to the 2nd floor to prep me for the monitors. CJ was on duty, so she found me and came in, "I saw your name come across the screen and my heart started beating fast," talking to my stomach and talking to the baby. "You better stay in there. We don't need any scare tactics. It's too early."

The attending nurse got me hooked to the monitor. My blood pressure was high, and the baby wasn't really moving! I kept myself calm, then I started to feel her flip around. It gave me an easy mind! Normally, I would vent to CJ, but this time it was the opposite. I let her pour as she told me a few things. I listened and I told her I was going to pray for her, and I did silently before drifting off to sleep.

The beeps from the monitor were going off because baby girl was kicking, moving, doing everything. The nurse said my baby was doing fine, "You two are going to be okay. Your blood pressure is down. They're are going to discharge you."

When I got home, I instantly went into worry mode because it was getting close to time to have my daughter and I have absolutely nothing. I didn't have to work that day, so we went to corporate prayer service. One of the ministers asked me if I was having a boy or girl. "Girl."

She said, "I got some stuff for you."

I'm sitting there scratching my head. I simply thanked her and Thank God for making ways out of no way. While my husband left me, God was there all the time.

Due to my health during this pregnancy, my work hours were being cut extremely low. I called Roman to let him know I needed extra money to get bills paid because my check wasn't enough. He told me he didn't live there anymore so he will not be helping me, and he never sent me anything.

While playing the word game, I put together the word **HOPE**. Did you know hope keeps us alive and gives us reassurance that we can make it even in the midst of our storms? When we feel like giving up, we search for hope. We connect hope with faith and link it to the word of God to supersede and strategize how life will be better.

My doctor gave me the notice to stop working because things were getting serious with my pregnancy and he didn't want me to lose my child. I informed my manager and I asked her about the two weeks' notice. She said that wasn't needed if I didn't plan on coming back, so I didn't worry about it. I did what I needed to do, typing up my letter and sending it to the headquarters. I loved my job, but my time was up. I couldn't keep risking my health, plus I knew this was God removing me. I let my job go, now I'm "**Venting For Trust**" *(T)o (R)ealize Yo(u)r (S)upport is (T)imely we have to trust God with everything even when it hurts. Sometimes we find ourselves doubting what the master can do. Take the limits off of God. He is the increase to your decrease. My heart is all in for God. My mind is focused on* *his goodness. The only thing for me to do is praise my way through while in the process of trusting him even when IT HURTS!*

I started to pray for my husband, keeping him covered even though we were in a bad place. My duties as a wife still remained. I texted him a sincere heartfelt message because even if we never go forward in the marriage we still need to build a relationship for our unborn child. I just felt it was the right thing to do. The bible states in **Proverbs 8:34 "Blessed is the man that hear me watching daily at my gates, waiting at the post of my doors."**

Sometimes we get ahead of God and rush into things quickly. I believe if Roman and I had taken things slower and gotten to know one another on more than one level, we could have been something great. He said God sent me to him, but what if he was just my assignment and not my husband. Things have turned out so bad for us. We haven't been married for long and I'm facing everything on my own; operating as a single parent but I'm a wife. It doesn't make a bit of sense. I never thought I would experience such trauma in my marriage. I hope things can get better and I can move forward and forgive him. At this point, however, I'm bitter, angry, suicidal, depressed, frustrated, and slipping away from God. This child needs us both even my other children as well. I grew up without my mother and father and he grew up without his father.

We can break the generational curse of being single parents and/or co-parents.

I'm in the situation I was in two pregnancies ago. The thing that hurt the most with this is I'm married and going through it alone. When vows were made before, God was it all an act? When he spoke those words out of his mouth, especially FOR BETTER OR WORSE. And when worse came, my husband walked out on me with no remorse, leaving the family to suffer.

My kids and I faced the holidays alone. It seems as if no one cares, or no one loves me like they confess out of their mouths. Sometimes I feel that no one is ever there for me the way I am there for them. It took me all the way back to my childhood. How I suffered from neglect, abandonment, lack of attention, love, acceptance, and the list goes on and on. The hurt from all of that is attached to the hurt I'm now experiencing in my marriage. Past hurt mixed with future hurt. I'm in a place where I have to **PACE** myself in life. The healing takes a lot longer than you'd expect.

I'm in need of a fast but of course, I can't do without food because of my pregnancy. There are other things that are distracting so I prayed to God and he gave me a challenge to start on another book. For these last three months, he wanted me to write with consistency. I didn't write anything during my pregnancy because of my job and dealing with other issues. I started on my 3rd Book, *"Dare to Seek,"* a prayer devotional. The first prayer I wrote was called 'Healing Leaf'

Dear, Father, give us a healing leaf that it may soften our hearts, soothe our minds, replenish our spirits, and to be more like you and less of ourselves. Because only you can bring a change where we lack and only you can fill where we are empty. We can't hide the hurt nor handle it. Help us to remind our soul to depend on your love to make us whole.

When I began to write, every burden I had was lifted from me. My freedom and strength is not only in God's house but in my writing as well. It hurts to heal but if there's no challenge how could we ever master the skill.

This year is about to end, and I want to go into the New Year FREE. I harbored tears, pain, hurt, disappointments, mistreatment, rejection, loneliness, and abuse. Everything went from sweet to sour. I'm ready for something new and fresh. I'm so tired of carrying this load (baby). This journey has been HELL! (H)urt (E)ffecting my (L)iving causing (L)oneliness. Nevertheless, I truly thank God for keeping me in it, even when I wanted to 'check out.' God said not so. I'm now in the position to wait on my freedom to come because there has been so much trying to destroy me. When we find the replacement to walk in all the things of God, he shows us that we can come out of anything.

We just have to keep our eyes on him so his victory can reign.

The minister from the church's daughter blessed me with clothes. I really thank God for my church family. They start the blessings off and leaving room for God to do more with their prayers. I picked my bible, turning it to *Isaiah 58* reading the whole chapter, and the verses that grab my attention were *4-6, Behold, ye fast for strife and debate, and to smite with the fist of wickedness: ye shall not fast as ye do this day, to make your voice to be heard on high. Is it such a fast that I have chosen? A day for a man to afflict his soul. Is it to bow down his head as a bulrush, and to spread sackcloth and ashes under him? Wilt thou call this a fast, and an acceptable day to the Lord? Is not this the fast that I have chosen to loose the bands of wickedness, to undo the heavy burdens, and to let the oppressed go free, and that ye break every yoke?*

I'm just blown because this is confirmation from when I spoke about going on a fast. I fasted from social media, phone, people, and television. I really wanted to stay focused on my assignment. God gave me a deadline to push and stretch soon, I will be giving birth to my 3rd book and 3rd baby.

I'm back on fire in my writing. It feels good to keep up with my challenge. I'm focused, I'm determined, I'm free to release all God has downloaded in me to help others and myself. I drifted off to sleep. Waking up to missed calls and messages from Roman.

All of sudden he's worried about the baby. Man look at this BS right here. I haven't heard from this man since we parted ways, now you want to act as if you are concerned. Please go on. You left so stay gone. I don't want to have anything to do with you! Is what I texted back!

Every time I talked to him, he reminds me so much of all the hurt he caused me. This is the time I'm trying to heal, and he comes to destroy me even more. I'm fasting but I failed the test. I have hatred in my heart for this man, and every chance I got, I was exploding on him. Saying whatever comes to my mind! I tried so hard to stay in a righteous character, but my fleshed started to rise up and my anger took completely over. I'm acting really FOOLISH! I begin to weep because I know I'm disappointing God. *Sigh.* I need to get it together and stop letting this man get the best of me.

Finally, Watch Night came. We enter into the presence of God. That's all I longed for. Just to get in the house to grab a taste of the atmosphere. I was bottled up with so many mixed emotions. Tears began to fall without my permission, and I cried the whole service, just worshipping God. I felt everything that I was going through breaking off of me. God is still stripping, shaping, and molding me to his perfection. I came in with my bucket(s) empty but now I'm getting them filled while worshipping him.

I got my seed prepared to sow. All I had was $80. With no hesitation, I SOWED IT! I needed so much from God on a personal level. I pray all the time for wisdom, knowledge, and how to love people like he loves them. I need to stay grounded in him.

The clock strikes 12 midnight and it is now 2018! MIRACLE, SIGNS AND WONDERS, the year of limitless, *"NO LIMITS NO BOUNDARIES.* In this season, I'm serving God limitless. Whatever he needs me to do, I will obey him promptly to get the task done. More importantly, get back to him to become closer; not setting boundaries but going over the boundaries to be guided more to Christ. My Pastor was instructing us what to do on our corporate fast. I was amazed; more confirmation for me. So, I have to stick with this fast to strengthen my spirit.

I'm so over this pregnancy. We have made another year and I'm still walking around and wobbling like a penguin. I am HUGE! This baby is wearing me down. I don't know if I can make it. I am exhausted.

When I returned home, I prepared something to eat. I ate but couldn't finish it. I threw up everywhere. I was so sick and dizzy. I had to hurry and lie down. I begin to pray, and God said **TUNE IN** while he's ministering to my spirit. He is helping me naturally with my body. It got extremely calm, as I felt myself go into an easy rest in him. I felt God touch my body. I felt like I was floating. Something I encountered when I was first saved, and I kept hearing the word, "tune." He said:

This year, keep your ears and eyes open, be tuned into everything, people around you, things that try to attack you or come against you. Be tuned in; I will show you how to hear and see on another level.

I got up to turn the fan on because it was so hot. I was sweating terribly. The fan blew my bible open to the book of Daniel landing my eyes on Chapter 10. Reading the whole chapter, verses 8-10 stuck on me, *Therefore I was left alone, and saw this great vision, and there remained no strength in me: for my comeliness was turned in me into corruption, and I retained no strength. Yet heard I the voice of his words: and when I heard the voice of his words, then was I in a deep sleep on my face, and my face toward the ground. And, behold, a hand touched me, which set me upon my knees and upon the palms of my hands.*

I read those scriptures and went into deep worship because God was just dealing with me about being tuned in and all that I experienced was in the word. My God, My God. He is worthy!

I get my last two pregnancy shots and I'm done. THANK YOU JESUS! God will take us through so much to only build us for who he needs us to be. I tried my hardest to run from the pain in my pregnancy, in my marriage, I mean everyday life. I'm not fond of pain, but pain has purpose. My pain showed me that no matter how bad it hurts, God was there, soothing and massaging me back to healing. All that I tried to dismiss, God kept it in my sight to feel it, see it, grasp it, and grieve it.

Pain prepares you for what's to come. Life doesn't stop your pain, you learn and grow in it to show others that God's glory is on your life; that you choose to be bold to tell as a testimony someday. In this season, it is the Lord. Therefore, I will not apologize for the person I'm becoming in him (God). Dysfunctional is powerful because it is so comfortable, and it takes so much to come out of it. I was born into a dysfunctional family but the "LOST ME" is committed to being found.

CJ called to tell me she had some clothes for the baby, and we would have a lunch date soon. I thank her for always thinking of my kids and me. She is truly a blessing to my family. When we get off the phone, it rings again. It's my husband calling, telling me he moved to another state and he had a job. I'm thinking, *how is that benefiting me, when you are living with someone.* Then I said what I was thinking to him. He goes into an uproar so now he has pissed me off.

"I'm trying my best not to lose it because it's crazy that you are trying to get up on your feet, helping someone else pay bills, and left your family suffering and struggling. This stuff is getting on my nerves! You got to stop running from your responsibilities. It's bad enough you have missed out on everything dealing with my pregnancy."

I can feel myself about to go in on him, so I calm myself down. Praying to God, asking him to take control over my thoughts because my smart mouth is ready to let loose! "This stuff is sickening. I'm tired of being nice. I'm about to introduce you to the sour side (the old Skyye)."

He hung up in my face, sending me a picture message of Divorce papers.

I said, "Yes. Please send the papers. In fact, bring them here so I can sign them."

He didn't text back.

I don't believe in divorce, but the way this marriage is going, we want last long. Everything has gone downhill for sure. I can't blame anyone but myself because I didn't seek God too much on him because I just knew he was IT! This is not how marriage is supposed to go. We are now living apart in two different cities. I'm lying there in tears and I hear God say: **You are in it now you have to go through it**. A lot of things we bring upon ourselves. Roman turned on me once he married me, now I'm carrying his baby that he left me to raise alone. I have to put on my *big girl* panties to see what the end is going to be. This can really mean *until death do us apart*. It's going to be me killing him or him killing me. I have had enough of the abuse. This is not love, and I know God isn't pleased with what is going on.

Time is closer, and baby girl will be here soon. I'm so nervous. My body was so tired, I kept saying that I'm not going to church, but God tugged on my broken heart. In *Psalms 56:3, "What time I am afraid, I will trust in thee."*

God is close to the broken hearted and I need to be repaired. I pressed my way, crying, feet swollen, hurting. As soon as I made it in the door, a wind of his glory touched my heart. I felt the pain cracking away from my heart. He touched my whole body. I couldn't explain if I wanted to, but I felt brand new.

We had first of the month Thursday Service. I sowed my seed and my pastor prayed for me. He said your birthing season is now. You are going to have this baby sooner than your due date, (*which was February 14, 2018, a scheduled C- Section*). She will not be premature. She will come out full-term. All of her organs will be working properly. She will make her grand entrance healthy and whole. He laid hands on me and I felt the power of God all through my body. When I left, I was so high in the spirit, I rest all that night and that next day!

I woke up at 1:00 that evening, getting a message from CJ telling me to meet her at our favorite eating spot for our lunch date. I got up, put some clothes on, and headed out the door. Outside, I looked up and there was a blue bird and a white and gray bird sitting in the corner of the bricks, looking at me. God said those birds sit there night and day being a watchman!

I never paid attention to those birds until God spoke to me about them. I made it to the restaurant, and I started to hurt really bad under my stomach, but I ignore it. I see CJ walking, so I wobble over to where she is, and we walk in the building and sit down. We catch up on a lot that's going on in life. I didn't vent too much because I felt the tears coming so I cut it off. She pulled a bag of clothes out for the baby. I just simply thanked God.

We ate good but had to cut our lunch date short because she had to get back to work. I got in the car and I cried. It was unbelievable that the blessings were still flowing. I made it home and the birds were still sitting. When I got in the house, they flew off! I was like, wow.

I could not sleep that night, so I finished the food I had left over from the restaurant. I tossed and turned all night, finally dozing off to sleep. While I'm sleeping, I didn't dream, but I hear a hospital beep (it was a signal of God trying to alarm me). I woke up the next morning cleaning my whole house. I was about to get breakfast started when I caught a sharp pain that had me breathing extremely fast. I had to sit down. I went to use the bathroom and I saw a little taste of blood mixed with some jelly looking sticky stuff in the stool. I called

CJ instantly and she said it's the mucus plug. IT'S TIME! I'll be there in five minutes, but she got here faster than 5 minutes. She helped me get my clothes on and while I was getting my son ready, she got us in the car.

While driving to the hospital, she was on the phone with the hospital getting my paperwork ready. We made it, and the staff rolled me to ER putting my admission ID band on while I signed the papers. They pushed me to the 2nd floor, put me on the monitor and I'm having contractions back to back, not feeling any pain. CJ sit there with me. She was off duty and I did not intend for her to be at work on her off day, but I knew she didn't mind because she comforted me the whole time she was there. I had one big crazy contraction and she came to rub my head and hands saying, "You are doing fine. We're going to get through this. I am here with you. Now I have been in labor for two plus hours.

I called Roman. He showed no concerns. He wasn't trying to get here. He made excuses the entire time we were on the phone. To keep from getting upset, I hung up and texted him a long message. I couldn't understand for the life of me why he would miss the birth of his first child. I started to have cold sweats; the nurse came in checking on me and I still hadn't dilated.

I'm getting furious because I have to get cut open for the third time. The clock is ticking, and time is scrolling on by. Now I have been in labor for six hours straight. The nurse came in to check me again saying you have dilated 5 and 1/2 centimeters, we have to get you prep for surgery. CJ clocked in to assist her. They put me on the other bed and as they roll me down to the surgery room, CJ is holding my hand because she knows I'm scared to death! They get me on the table for surgery. They prep for my cesarean and I get a shot in my spine to numb my body from my stomach to my toes. This time I would be awake to hear the baby cry. Something I didn't experience with my first two pregnancies, so I'm nervous.

During the surgical procedure, CJ was holding my hand and holding me still, keeping me calm. She talked to me in my ear. She must have felt me going crazy in the head, but her words eased my heart rate. After the procedure, they laid me back carefully, but I can't feel anything my anxiety kicks in, I'm staring at the lights drifting in and out I'm sure I'm about to meet Jesus I'm losing my wind, but I didn't mention it. I called on Jesus. He gave me a second wind. I took a deep breath, but I'm getting frustrated because I can't feel my feet. Now my depression has kicked in. My mind is clouded, my heart is racing. I said, Lord, you got to help me. Tears are rolling down my face. When it felt like my heart was about to explode from the frustration, I heard my baby cry. It was so beautiful; that day I cried with her too!

February 3, 2018, I welcomed Reign Trinity in the world. When they brought her to my face, I cried even louder and whispered to her, "Thank you for saving my life."

The anxiety eased away, the depression went mild, and my heart rate returned to normal. They got me into recovery and the awakening of Reign's birth not only allowed me to survive the cut but death too. As she slept peacefully on my chest, there was no way I could. The emotional ties of the maternity wounds swept over me and more tears poured from my eyes.

Until you see things God's way with unnecessary dealings of being sane in this season, your circumcision will not be healed. Moving past the pain is the difficult part. I'm in desperate need of God. My cut reminded me not to get complacent and don't but allowed me to get prepared through anything the assurance of power, relieve, recycle, and replenishing.

Reign is here, but still no Roman. I'm calling him to see if he was still coming. He didn't come. I'm fed up with all this mess, but I sent him pictures anyway and even to his mom. I tried to get out of bed to walk, but I fell back. This pain is crazy. I asked God for strength because I had to get up in order to heal properly. I got to Reign bed and pulled up with all the muscles I had! I walked down the hall hurting so bad, but I focused on Reign's beauty. God spoke, saying, **there is pain in your beauty.**

Time after time, we want to make things pretty without going through something, but the beauty is labor, hard work, birth, sacrifices, and risking life to give life. I discovered that the beautiful chaos was my marriage, my assignments, my pregnancy, and God kept me in it all. The pain stripped me, the marriage is breaking me, the assignment is building me, and Reign is helping me flourish into destiny.

I got a call from Roman's mom. She acts like she is concerned, but I know it's all a front. The woman doesn't even like me. I saw it all through her spirit. She asked for a DNA TEST! I tried to stay as calm as I could because of the surgical, and I was in the process of healing. I said, "I didn't sleep with you, I slept with my husband, and if he wants a blood test he can come get one himself!"

She continued talking. CJ heard her and is pissed. Never had I witnessed that side of CJ before. She took my phone and hung up on Roman's mom. I called my aunt, and she called Roman's mom, putting her on 3-way. Not knowing I'm on the phone, Roman's mom is talking about me like a dog. I wanted to unmute the phone so bad, but God has to fight this battle. My aunt put her in her place, but when I get well *it's on* is what I'm thinking. I'm tired of these demons trying to attack me through people. I called my husband and went off on him. I can't stand him at this point. The hatred for him is turning me evil. I'm praying to God and I'm asking him over and over to protect me. I hate drama, I love my peace, but I'm sucked dry from it.

The time came for me to leave the hospital and I'm ready to go home to my own comfort. I facetime Zion so she can see Reign and she was so happy saying, "Ma, she is so pretty."

My son, not so happy. His godmother brought him up to see me. He wasn't having it. He had a complete meltdown right there. It hurts my heart because this is going to be a big adjustment for him, but he won't be alone. I had to get adjusted to adding another baby to the family, raising three kids as a whole. I'm puzzled trying to figure out schedules of what will take place at home when I needed to be focused on getting healed. But the devil was on the loose, and I knew God was about to clear the space of what is about to be born in my life.

I have grown discouraged by the hardships. I have to provide. I'm tired of struggling, and this unnoticed rock of me being hidden made it difficult to see my purpose because I was focused on the problem. I have a calling for a reason, and I'm still searching to find the way.

I was hurting so bad from all that took place and the pains from my cut is getting the best of me. I pulled my prayer journal out, writing to release what is bothering me: *Dear, God, I'm asking for divine healing right now from all past hurts that's trying to creep back on me emotionally, physically, and mentally. I'm trying to stay focused on you. You can have all of me. I want none of me. Life is tearing me down. I need you right now in this hour to lift me from anything that's trying to destroy me. You are here with me. I ask that you keep me covered, my children, my family even my husband, as we go through our separation. Allow your favor to still reign on him. I love you, Jesus with all my life. Amen* ☺

I face-timed Roman so he could see Reign, he didn't seem happy, so I just told him I would talk with him another time. I felt in that moment, God is really about to expose the hidden things of which Roman is hiding. I know something is up because I feel so uneasy in my spirit. What hurts me the most is knowing that my child is only bonding with me and not her father I begin to weep for Reign

I grew up without both of my parents I never had a great relationship I have tried to build but could never stick with it. I'm so afraid for her I'm beating myself up mentally because I don't know where have I went wrong I did the right thing to marry going into it with true love, going by the principles of being a wife as the bible states but in all I got is abuse, I hurry to wipe my face as the nurse came in to check my vitals, shortly after that CJ came in and she helped me out the bed, walking me into the bathroom helping me wash up in areas I couldn't reach, she sat there spending time with me, soothing me I was so appreciative of that. I begin to thank God for seeing me through my surgery as I rub my staples on my stomach I felt my scar still split some areas were tender, some areas were hard not all areas were healed. We can be like that in life. In some areas, you can hurt so bad from the wound being split open to where the tenderness aches. To make the pain worst, we pick at the scar constantly, allowing it to bleed instead of healing.

It was time for us to go home. Reign's godmother and friend came to bless Reign with a car seat and an outfit. Following up with CJ blessing us with a baby bag and a bag full of clothes. I couldn't stop the tears from flowing. I was discharged to go home, and it felt good to be back in the atmosphere of which I set, along with the presence of God. As I walked in the door of my house, a sudden peace came over my body. CJ helped us get settled in, making sure we had everything in order before she left. I received a text from Roman's mom saying, please forgive me. I never responded. I looked at the phone, throwing it aside to continuing on what I was doing.

Because my body was swollen (and my hands were even worse), I had to remove my wedding ring; not being able to wear it my whole pregnancy. I'm pondering if should I put it back on since I had discovered infidelity in my marriage. When I decided to put it back on, my finger started to hurt even more. I'm like Lord, what is this? I snatched the ring off and laid it back on the kitchen counter where it had been laying for five months. My heart was at ease as I walked out of the kitchen. I strongly believe God is about to remove Roman from me. He texted, wanting to make things right. I'm focused on getting well. I don't care if you come back or not is what I texted back.

I picked up my bible, and turning to Daniel 4, I read the whole chapter. The words that grabbed my attention were *a great feast, queen by reason, understanding and wisdom, excellent spirit, and knowledge.* God began to minister saying:

In this season of your life, you will encounter a great feast, not only in your family but in your spirit as well. You will be fed plenty of bread loaves and more loaves, never running out, getting full off of everything I give you, not wanting or needing anything. You are the queen by reason. You have your crown which is property put upon. What reason you have is to stand in freedom for you will go far with me, even when everyone else would try to destroy your mind. You understand that life without wisdom cannot be displayed as you flourish in your excellent spirit using knowledge to get people to come to Christ. I affirm you. I command you to walk in your calling and in your assignment, for only I know what your purpose holds. Keep your eyes on me. I can take you when others can't help you find the way.

I fell asleep, waking up to a knock on the door. It's CJ and her mother with MORE items. I cried and cried. Reign had so much stuff that the closet was filled, and I had to place her items in my computer room. I didn't have enough room to receive all that God was pouring. Not only that, I had a check in the mailbox, I don't know where it came from, didn't try to find out, but what God ministered to me was in FULL EFFECT! I wasn't healed enough to go back to church, but I made sure I paid my tithes by sending them.

God spoke to me that night saying sow a seed of $1,000.00 out of the $1,500.00 check that I received. I didn't hesitate. I sealed it in a tithe envelope, obeying what he said. So, I could plant it for next Sunday, I called my apostle to pick it up since I couldn't be there.

My recovery is coming along, so I'm able to move around the house just a little. I started to reorganize and noticed my other kids lacking a lot of stuff while Reign was gaining more stuff, but I didn't let that distract me. I knew what God spoke to me, and he will bless them when it is time. I sent pictures of Reign to Roman's phone. He said he would be back home to make things work; he wanted me back. I said ok whatever.

I got a knock on the door. It was church members stopping by, doing a follow up. They gave me a gift bag, a fruit basket, and a card that read: *I want to let you know you're in our prayers and to remind you that although life brings many changes, God's love for us remains constant. No matter what you are facing, we love you much, House of Prayer (FAP).*

That touched my heart and healed a few of my wounds. I needed those words in ways they couldn't even imagine.

My husband came back home. I take it he was already on the road. All issues we had, I swept under the rug to focus on the kids, especially Reign, hoping she was the glue to get us closer and keep our bond intact.

This was Roman's first time seeing her and holding her. It was a priceless moment to share sitting as a family again. I got in the shower, and I prayed to God to open my eyes more. I had to cut my shower short because the baby was crying; he left her unattended in the room. I stepped outside and he was smoking. Whatever it was, he chunked it. You didn't tell me you were a smoker and I started to go off on him about Reign. He knew he was caught, so he didn't have time to make up a lie. He went to the bathroom, so I went through his phone and he's still talking to the woman that wrote to me about him a while back. "Why are you still talking to her?"

"What are you talking about?"

I'm trying to regain control with myself because I'm about to start swinging on him. "YOUR BESTFRIEND," I yelled as I put the phone in his face to show him what they were talking about via text message. Even after I saw what they were talking about, he still lied. I walked off, letting it go my body couldn't handle the stress of fighting while being in recovery, and I didn't want the baby to wake up.

Nothing really had changed. I asked God to expose him, but I can't take it! I'm depressed. "How can you say you love God, but treating me like I'm nothing?"

"I'm SORRY, SKYYE! What else you want me to do. LEAVE?"

Everything that was hidden is coming out back to back. I wrote to her. I just couldn't ignore the voices in my head nagging me to give her a piece of the old me. **I have a heart, and I have a family. Why are you constantly messing with my husband?"**

Instead of writing me back, she wrote an indirect post about me, so I just stop talking to her. As if God knew that the pain was washing over me, tears streamed down my face as the voices got louder to give her a piece of my mind. Roman came to me confessing. Sitting in front of me, he admitted that he had an affair. I AM NUMB! I have no words to utter. I cried fresh tears to add to the fresh pain. I cried for the woman whose eyes were blind to all that is coming. I cried for the safety of walls I built that didn't protect me from the searing pain. I cried for the broken pieces of myself that I buried in false love while trying to be repaired. I lost my joy, my peace, my hope, and my belief in a marriage that wasn't worth fighting for. This war is ongoing, and far from over.

I cried every day allowing the pain to bleed through my tears. No matter how many tears fell, I knew that my eyes would dry while the pain will still be watering my wounds and scars of all that I went through and would be going through.

I was released from recovery, while my body was healing still from carrying Reign, my marriage was suffering from wounds that were already ruined through hurt, rejection, abandonment, lies, and abuse that needed to be repaired and amended by God.

I didn't say anything to Roman I didn't have words, plus I didn't have the energy to accept more lies and the fake apologies. He was guilty, so he tried to rebuild, well at least attempt to connect back with me. He seemed committed to fixing the broken bond between us, but I wasn't hopeful. I didn't have the strength to end the marriage----- or to save it. I was flying on broken wings, praying we'd fly together in UNITY. The conversations reached a dead end of pure silence. We weren't talking at all since the recent suspicions I carried. He can no longer be trusted. I will be in a very bad space to question everything he does all because of the deceit. He asked me to forgive him. I didn't say anything, I just burst into tears.

I'm finally recovered from my surgery, and we can attend church. Life was so crazy, I needed an extra dose of God's presence and his strength to carry me on through. My faith is wavering, and I need to hear a fresh word. We got to church. I owe God a ridiculous praise, I sat down nine months due to my pregnancy, and I'm ready because he deserves it.

Roman reconnected back with the ministry, getting a new start to change, I guess, but what good did it do. When we left church, we got into the car arguing, in which he started. I'm so sick of him. I put the "Saved Skyye" to the side to introduce him to the "Old Skyye." I'm tired of him treating me any kind of way. Everything he did to me, I did to him, revengefully. He talked crazy to me, I ate him up with my words too. He didn't treat me like a wife, so I stop acting like one. He said, "You're operating in the wrong spirit, my mother warned me about you."

I said, "You and your mammy can go to hell! When you want your clothes washed and food on the table, that's who you need to be calling or taking a trip to see."

I stopped doing all of my duties. I found myself abusing him with my words, to show him how it felt, now we are sailing in an abusive marriage! He got on the phone talking extremely bad about me, and I went off on him and the person that was listening to the lies he was telling. "TRY ME NOW! I'm not carrying your child. I will bust you in your face and be ready for your family too."

He got mute! Him reconnecting with the ministry was only a front. This man is letting the devil use him, and I have let the devil use me too. There's nothing godly about him. I'm starting to see him for who he is spiritually. What have I gotten myself into? Then I thought about that prophecy that was spoken and I didn't really heed because I was trying to protect my husband.

While he continued to pretend, it was true that I was in love with a liar. I didn't listen. I stayed to try to make the marriage work, things got worse. I prayed to God that things could get better, but he kept being a liar! I calmed all the way down, God had broken me right in the middle of my mess because I was about to do something evil to my husband. I cried to release the anger, and whatever hurt he caused at that moment. God said to repent and ask him to forgive you. I did what he said, but I'm so filled up with bitterness, hurt, and pain. Roman didn't accept my apology, calling me fake. I want to kill this man, but he isn't worth me going to jail to leave my kids behind to suffer. I got before God in prayer:

Dear, God, help me to forgive like you, to love like you, to be more like you, to be more like the word. I'm all yours. Sometimes I fall short of your Glory but help me God when I can't keep myself. God you are Alpha and Omega. You know the way, you know the truth; help me to walk in it.

Help me to see Christ as you do. I just want to love and do things your way. I know I have acted out fleshly. Please forgive me, Lord, and help me to do better. Amen.

I'm lying there disgusted and sobbing more. I'm out of my mind. I'm trying to gain a heart to forgive him, but it is so hard when he keeps mistreating me. Our 1st Anniversary is coming up, and over the year, I encountered so much pain. We had a service, and the topic was "How to Survive Your Storm?" As my apostle gives us the bread of life, I took notes. When I summarized the message, I got this from it:

The Winds can become storms, coming without warnings out of nowhere. There are some things you will learn in the storm that you couldn't see until you come out. These storms will come to make it difficult to give up and when you feel like that, start fasting; it bothers the enemy. I'm like, Wow! The message hit home.

I'm hurting, and I don't think it's fair that I have to face this in my marriage. It's not easy. I need help, I need strength and God's Agape Love. I'm in a place where I wanted to give up on everything and everybody. I am tired, God. Come on in to see about me before I'm meeting you sooner than my time.

In this season, I have to be PROCESSED. The process is for imperfect people. There are no short cuts in God. He will not remove you but keep you in the process to get you along while being on the journey to your will for his life.

The pain tolerance is to get you to your destiny while your emotions reach maturity when you're in the process. He cuts the time in half. Set yourself aside in this season to fast and pray. Allow the wilderness to release a process so you can make up his promise as he strips you to take you where he is trying to get you to. You have to go through it because every environment is not concluding to your process. It will make it premature.

We survived the one year, BARELY! It is still filled with injuries, still suspiciously thinking here's infidelity, abuse, and so much other stuff. Roman said. "HAPPY ANNIVERSARY," I said it back with no excitement because I'm unhappy, and there wasn't anything to be happy about, but he did show me a good time. We packed up to get on the road to Georgia for the rest of the week. I really didn't want to go because of the way his mom treated me. She never knew anything about me, but she judged me from a lot of things Roman had said. I was distant from her as well, but she needed to meet her granddaughter. So, I gambled, going even if it hurts, but I'm still in no place to forgive her or her son.

We got on down the road, and we aren't talking at all. For a whole hour straight, we were silent until I sparked up a conversation. That didn't go so well. We got into a heated argument. I got on my phone and focused on Reign to keep me smiling. Life is a journey many miles away from where you want to go. Roman and I are lost on this path (our marriage); we want to call it quits, we're on the brink of divorce, but neither one of us believed in it. We have kids involved which makes the decision so much harder.

I'm sitting in the back seat crying and hoping to be free from all this madness. "I forgive you, Roman," I said so calmly, while my heart begged to differ. Holding on to the abuse that has me traumatized to even live.

"I forgive you too. You have to know things won't get better if we're always at each other throats."

This drive is irritating me. I played games on my phone and stayed attentive to Reign to keep me sane. I gave my whole life to Roman even while he abused me. I still wanted to make things work. I felt like he could have changed but only if he stops playing the victim and blaming me for his screw-ups. We stopped at a store to get gas, and he asked if I wanted anything to eat. I said no but he brought me something anyway. I took it to be nice. However, we got back on the highway, and he is speeding, and I am going off because we have an infant in the car and we most definitely don't have money to give to the police. I kept telling him to slow down. He isn't listening to anything I say so I eased my seatbelt on. As soon as I clicked it, I look up and see police lights. I'm sitting praying. The officer came to the window and he lied to the officer. I'm sitting in the back seat just listening to how good of a liar he is. he talked the man out of a ticket. Giving him a warning, the officer let him go.

Then God reminded me of how he manipulated me with his words and when he couldn't get his way, he would take the anger out on me with abuse. I sat there pondering and God began to speak, saying: **There is more, but I have to prepare your heart for what is next.**

Welcome to Georgia.

We made it to the house. Going in, his mom reached out to give me a hug. I hugged her back but felt so awkward, so I handed her Reign. She didn't seem happy about Reign. As I paid attention to his mom's body language, she was checking her more than anything. I got Reign from her because I don't like her spirit. She started to switch. I see now she's a pretender like her son. God insists that I help her clean. I said, *God, this isn't what I came here for.* God said, *You are down here on an assignment not for an anniversary.*

Often, we can't always do what we love, and we have to help people that secretly hate us. All the time, God has me to do things as such, and I never have seen him forsaking my blessing for blessing the enemy. I did what he said, and Roman's mom and I got to talking. She started to warm up; me, I'm still observing. She said, Wow, you are nothing like my son described you to be. I just smiled because only if she knew her son, she wouldn't be siding with him. She pretended to like me the whole time I was there. I went with it. Roman mentioned something about ministry and I'm like I didn't come here for that. "I will minister Sunday night?"

"WHAT... so you are telling me I have to miss church when we had plans to leave that Saturday. ARE YOU SERIOUS?" It was never about the anniversary. It was about supporting him when all he has ever done was speak negativity about my books. Not buying them, nor supporting me with them, but drag me to Georgia to support him. We went on out to enjoy the rest of the day. We got back to the house because I wasn't feeling well. He came out of the kitchen with wine and I'm like, I'm not drinking that, and he tried to make me drink it. I pushed the cup so hard it spilled on his clothes. He is so controlling and demanding, he is really trying me, and I'm trying my best to be on my best behavior. I just left it alone.

He drove me over to see my niece and nephew and my sister so they all could see Reign. It would be their first time seeing her. We were so happy to see one another. I don't see them often, so I cherish every second. Even though we are miles apart, the distant never stop the love from flowing. Roman rushed me, so I had to go ahead and leave to keep confusion down. We made it to his mom's house, and she gave me her book to read. Her title hit home for me, "Abused,

Confused, and Misused." When I open it, I understand now why Roman acts the way he does. His father abused his mother for years. This is a generational curse; something deep-rooted in him. There was nothing I could do but pray. God would have to deliver him totally.

While I'm in a place of deliverance, I'm far from my healing. A lot of the issues have cursed this marriage. Even with myself from past hurts, childhood issues, and the insecurities that I have carried all my life. Man, we are jacked up and was nowhere near ready for marriage. We are unequally yoked in the spirit mainly from his lies and from my hurting. We are both wearing "SCARS" in need of (S)trength to (C)ome (A)vailable through (R)ighteousness to (S)ave us, but we were dismissing them; both of us bleeding, not going deeper in God but exceling in the pain.

I stopped praying for my marriage because I felt my prayers weren't being answered. In fact, things were getting worse. I knew I was lost. A part of me moved so far from out of God's will, and I could no longer find my way. I just hope it isn't too late to seek him more. No matter how rough the patches get, we can't avoid God. No matter how hard life gets, he is still there pulling on us trying to bring us out. There's this misconception that once you make it to a certain level in your life, you escape all problems and troubles. We are young and still have a lot of growing to do.

Skyye Howze

This pain had spread to the point we were both exhausted, angry, and emotionally bankrupt. I couldn't fake any signs of joy. I'm not good at pretending anyway. I stopped giving him the love he didn't deserve, and I know that probably pushed him further to other women but I'm at the point where I no longer care. The hurt has turned me into another person. When we learn to find peace in our season of suffering, our suffering will come to an end. I needed that more than ever. In my due time.

God doesn't just leave us in our misery to suffer. So often we look for him to calm everything, when we started the chaos, to begin with. But there are times God will choose you to trust him with the grace he provides to get you through the storm because we need the rain to shower on us. It will help us grow in areas where we hurt the most. I could no longer focus on the things that caused me to draw away from God. I NEEDED TO HEAL PROPERLY!

I flow into the poetic part of my soul, talking aloud so I can hear my own words fill me as the pain empties from me:

Who am I when I let pride destroy my life
What have I become in the hurt that tried to destroy me,
Life seems unbearable
As the pain tries to keep me in remembrance of my past.
Am I really walking in freedom,

Crowned Butterfly

*Or am I just seizing the moment to be free from a lot of
things?*
I feel like dying as the pressures of life hit me,
I'm serving God
I'm sacrificing
I'm obedient but still don't see a harvest
My patience is running thin
My faith is detouring
My life is a mess
I don't know if I'm coming or going
Everything in me wants to give up
But deep down in me
I still have a fight for victory.

Chapter Seven

Virtuously Evolved

I have a tattoo of a colorful butterfly on my right shoulder and when it would be seen many would ask what it means. "JESUS FREED ME," adding it also symbolizes the freedom that's in me I would say. I honestly forgot it was there when it once healed (A place I'm trying to reach). I got the tattoo when I was 17 years of age, not knowing how badly I would need it to reflect on my life back then to now. While my set position is to be crowned in the different colors of life. I dived in without my wings speeding, flying ,trying to get to my destination, and then I begin to fall without my wings; one flopping, trying to float back to the top with no force.

I'm panicking. Trying to vapor through the dry and smoky places because I need to be free from my past mistakes, hurt, and mainly everything that causes me to stop flying. This stuff makes no sense to me. I'm in a desperate place of "healing." It is needed because my marriage is being destroyed because of my past hurt along with his habits and addictions. I wanted my marriage to be my safe place, my refuge. Yet with the incident of another woman, the lies and betrayal, it was the inferno I could never escape. The girl in me who loves to chew ice obsessively had melted away, leaving a puddle of who she used to be to gain the new woman she knew she could be. So many curses are brought up on this marriage. I honestly don't know how we were still standing to begin with.

So, the night came for us to go to the event. I really didn't want to go. I felt uneasy the whole ride. We get to the place and I don't know these people. I'm looking around, standing off, but with respect, I speak because that is the polite thing to do. I sat quietly as my spirit discerned the rest. We got into the room where they were setting up. A guy gets up to preach. I couldn't even tell you what the sermon was about. It was just that boring. It was time to give an offering. I put my last $10.00 in the basket.

As they finished up with prayer and wrapping things up, I'm thinking, it's time to go. Not only that, it was getting late and I needed my baby to be home in the bed. I looked at Roman sideways and mad. If looks could kill, he would be dead. I found out they were doing Gospel Rap, so they got going with all the people who got up to do their songs and I'm not even paying attention. I could have stayed at the house for this; a bunch of nonsense. This event had no anointing anywhere in it.

Time was whining down and Roman was the last to Rap. He finished! As soon as he put the mic down, I yelled. "Roman. I'm ready to go." So, we got in the car and the argument became so furious, he cursed. "Wow, how you just finished rapping about the Lord but curse me out. You HYPOCRITE!" And then I just closed my mouth because if I say one more thing, we will be fighting.

We made it to the house. I didn't go to sleep. I stayed up all night to finish packing our luggage. Not only am I packing up everything, but I'm also packing up more hurt, more insecurities, more pain, more failure, and more unresolved issues. His mom handed us a bible on marriage with guides and keys to follow to have a healthier marriage.

Honestly, I didn't want to take it because all in the back of my mind I'm looking into getting a divorce when I get back home. With a fake smile, I said thanks, and we left about 6 that morning. Before getting on the road, we stop to get gas and coffee. I tried to make a phone call, but my phone was off, so I had to use his phone to check on my kids and to let them know I was on my way home.

We got on the road and I'm reading the bible out loud so he can hear as well. There was some deep stuff in it. I mean very helpful stuff to amend marriages, but my heart and mind was already stuck on the brokenness of the marriage. I WANT OUT!

The car started acting weird, so we pulled over to a nearby Walmart to check to see what was the problem. He found the problem as someone else helped him with the car. I saw WIFI available, so I wrote a few on Messenger to let them know my phone was off. However, I check my debit card and $150.00 was on it. When we left out to come to Georgia, I had 27 cents on it! Thank You, Jesus for being a provider. I didn't inform my husband that I had money because I know how wasteful he is with it! So, I just paid the phone bill, not making any calls but texting everyone to let them know my whereabouts and what was going on. We got on the interstate and the car started to run hot AGAIN!

So, we had to pull over to let the car cool down, then he started back driving. It is so much pressure, but we have to keep on driving (Pressing). The car problems got worst and I'm getting nervous because we have an infant in the car. I am going off to no end. I exploded. I didn't care if I hurt his feelings or not because he knew something was wrong with this car but lied to me like everything was good, still getting on the road, putting all our lives in danger.

See now he is playing with me. Our child is in this car and it is HOT! I never saw a man so irresponsible. He wasn't trying to call anyone, thinking he can do everything on his own. While we're arguing, we need to be praying I suppose. I called my cousin to tell him what was going on. He said he would try to figure something out. The car cooled down enough for us to make it to Alabama.

As soon as we got into Alabama, we were stuck. The car wouldn't crank. In fact, it stopped while he was driving. I screamed so loud, I'm crying, I'm frustrated because this child is in this car! Man, we sat there for almost two hours on the side of the freaking road. I called my cousin again telling him to come get us. "You have to help us. I need to get Reign home."

He said he was coming up with a plan and I needed to be patient.

I have completely lost my mind on Roman. I was filled with so much rage. Reign started to cry. I calm her down to console her and fan her with a piece of paper to keep her cool. She drifted off to sleep. I never in my life been in a drastic situation like this, so even if it was for a second or an hour, God humbled me in the midst of my rage. I got a chance to feel what it would be like if I was homeless. That's exactly what I felt like out on the road with no help from 6 that morning until about almost 4 that evening, with a newborn baby, car trouble, and my marriage turning for the worst.

I began to weep and weep to God and as I prayed to him it all reverted back to depending on him solely. Thinking I can depend on my husband, but he didn't fit the description at all. He was too selfish to do such! I asked Roman if he knew anyone in Alabama. He said he did! "Can you please call them to get us off this interstate."

He called the guy, and he and his wife came with no problem. I don't know these people, but my child needs to get out of this heat.

So, the guy's wife helped us get our bags and put them in her car, getting us to her house. I felt a little better, but my focus was getting home to my children and getting Reign and myself away from my husband. I was looking up bus tickets so Reign and I could get on the bus. "What are you doing Skyye?"

"I'm ready to go home!"

"NO, we would just have to stay the night here until we figure things out!"

"WHAT!!" But what choice did I have? God, what is going on? I need you now to calm my heart and my mind. I don't feel protected with this man. I want to strangle him. I feel alone, I'm afraid and all he is thinking about is himself. This man is too inconsiderate and selfish to be anybody's husband. Please remove him out of my life, God.

Even in the midst of what was taking place, God began to show me how he was taken from me. Not only mentally, physically, sexually and emotionally but with his finances too. He had money in his pocket that he didn't know I knew he had. He lied and said he didn't have money, asking me for what I had so I wouldn't get a bus ticket. I gave it to him anyway so they could fix the car.

My cousin called to check on us and he was relieved that we were off the interstate. We made it to the guy's house, and my spirit is so vexed! I just stayed to myself and played with Reign to keep my mind from off a lot. The guy's wife asked if I wanted anything to eat. I said no because I don't eat from everybody. I just asked for something to drink. "Water, perhaps."

Roman came in saying they fixed the problem and we would leave in the morning and even though the day was rough I still laid in his arms falling to sleep. I heard Reign cry and I jumped. She was hungry and needed a diaper change. I consoled her until she drifted back off to sleep. I decided to stay up to go into prayer before getting on the road, asking God to give us traveling grace.

The light peeped through the blinds alerting me that it's a new day. I shook Roman to let him know it was time to go. We got our things packed and headed down the road. I apologized to him for how I acted out of frustration, asking him to forgive me. I needed PEACE between us, but the pattern of pain kept reminding me of the hurt over and over again and making me extremely angry.

We made it into a further part of Alabama, and while getting ready to exit, the car quit again. I screamed, "I'M SO SICK OF THIS, ROMAN. I WILL NEVER GO ANYWHERE ELSE WITH YOU."

I failed the test of asking for forgiveness right there. He got out the car, slamming the door, pacing back and forth. God speaks, saying: *Daughter, you are about to exit all of what's trying to destroy you. You have traveled on the road of hurt, pain, disappointments, and mistreatment all your life. You are close to the exit and after you merge into the lane to see the exit sign, you will leave all nightmares behind, not returning back, but will be fulfilled with total healing and deliverance.*

Roman said, "I called a tow truck. They should be here in 15 minutes."

I called my cousin and he said he was on his way to me, and I did inform him that the tow truck would pull us to the nearest auto parts store. The tow truck came, we got in the tow truck, and I saw a Plaza with all different types of stores on it. I spotted this wing place. I hadn't eaten in two days. I checked my card and only had 1.27 cents on it after Roman used it to fix the problem with the car.

I went into the restaurant to the restroom to wash Reign up and put her on fresh clothes. When I came back out, there was food on the table. I went to the counter to thank the Asian woman who owned the wing place. There was no doubt this wasn't God. I was crying so I couldn't even eat, But I pulled myself together since I hadn't eaten in two days. I ate, but at the same time I was in deep thought, trying to come up with ways to divorce my husband. He interrupted my thoughts, coming in to check on us, then stepped back out to finish looking at the car.

My cousin finally pulled up. I couldn't be happier to see him. We got in the car and I instantly falls to sleep from being full from eating. I slept the whole drive. I was exhausted. When I woke up, we were almost in Cleveland. I thanked God for the traveling grace. The first trip I made was picking up my kids. They were so happy to see me, and I was too.

We got home, I unpacked and loved on my kids. I had to cut the time I was spending with them to get in preparation to do my motherly duties since they had school the next day. God began to show me an open vision of my husband and his best friend. I didn't say anything at that moment. I decided to wait until the next day. We got in bed and before long. it was the morning. I got the kids off to school. He asked me if I would take him a few places. I dropped him off to sell CDs.

When I got back home, I wrote her (best friend) and again, she denied it. Without any warning, text message or calls, I pulled back up on Roman. He hurried up and got off the phone. God had already shown me that's who he was faceciming. I still haven't said anything. He asked me to take him to the store. I said sure. He got out of the car not knowing his phone dropped out his pocket. I picked it up and went through it. Boom! Just as God showed me. The facetime ending time was still on the phone, so I went through the messages. They both are talking bad about me. He is telling her he's about to divorce me so they can get married. I laughed to keep from hitting him, but I was hurt to the core. I remembered the number in my mind. He got back in the car. "What's that in your pocket?"

"A pack of gum." He lied again.

I just drove on home. As soon as we got in the door, I got to talking. "God showed me an open vision of you and ole girl. I wrote her, and she denied it. So, what's going on?"

"You should trust me by now," he said. "We can't get better if you don't believe me. We have nothing going on. I'm telling the truth."

So, I know he is sick mentally because he is calling God a lie now. I called the number out. He's still lying. I repeated what I saw in the messages. Another lie added. He got so mad and said f**k you, Skyye and punched a big hole in the bedroom door. As the loud noise vibrates through the house, he scares Reign and she begins to scream and cry like I never heard before. I SAID GET OUT MY HOUSE NOW!

"You dumb b***h. You better be glad it isn't your face." Roman continued, "And I'm not going no d***n where."

In the heat of the arguments about him and her, he tried to make me feel crazy. What I couldn't accept that he was playing with my mind, and trying to make me go against what God had shown me. I was losing it over him, and it all was one big joke. Clearly, the joke was on me. What I learned in that very moment was that my husband was a "LIAR" just like it was prophesied to me, but I wanted to believe different in all of this.

Although I did ask God to remove Roman, I felt like leaving would break me. There was a part of me holding on to the treatment because I felt like it was all I deserved. It was in that very moment I was learning that I could still be used while being damaged to no end. We all know if we both are lost, you can't get no directions. The best thing to do is EXIT!

I feel so stupid. How was I blind to all of this? I mean no one knew how bad my marriage was because my business was my business, and even while I feared for my own life after he constantly made threats to kill me, but in it all, God was there. He protected me behind the walls of my home. I SURVIVED WHAT MOST DON'T COME OUT OF. I'm tired of being the bigger person. Eventually we decide to treat people the way they treat us. I felt the anger turn my heart black. They had to stop playing with me because my crazy side was on the rise to kill them both!

He promised me he would stop talking to her from the previous suspicions that I carried and reading those messages BROKE ME! He had more trust with his mistress than he did with his wife. As much as I wanted Roman to believe in our love. If I could be honest, I never believed in it myself. Just the love we were capable of achieving with all the lies and secrets. "Sigh" I go into my poetic flow to soothe what's trying to overtake me:

My heart is racing
I can't fathom the pain I'm facing
I'm in this journey,
I'm confused,
I can't stop worrying about life.
God, why did you choose me to be the vessel,
I've been going through hell
While seeking help to reach my destiny
All I want is better
These assignments are keeping me burdened
While my marriage is crumbling
I'm trying to get free,
So, I want to be bound in this season.
GOD WHERE ARE YOU?
I'm trusting you to bring me through this raging storm
I just want to be everything you called me to be,
But there's no way I can get there in all this fear
I'm trusting you,
But I feel overlooked as the pain controls my soul.

I did not want to live like this any longer. I accepted that I could not change him only God could. But I did use the last of hope I had left to become better

235

myself. In the end, I prayed that God's will be done. I just wished I would have asked him for the strength to handle whatever it was that was slowing me down from destiny. I felt like I'm the only one losing here. They lied. They cheated and conversed throughout our entire marriage. WHERE IS GOD IN ALL OF THIS? I'm confused.

I was giving Roman and this woman too much power. I challenged myself to move forward regardless of what I feel I lived in and what I lost. I express myself to God trusting him with my pain, overwhelming sense of thinking, anger, the infidelity in the marriage, and the ongoing abuse. My revengeful ways started to kick back in. I wanted to believe that they would reap what they have sown. I was bitter because I seem to be the only broken one in the whole situation. I wanted them to hurt just as bad as I was hurting and if I get a hold to any information, I'm exposing both of them. I didn't care if he stayed or left. My focus was getting back in my rightful place with God. But he ends up leaving.

I started this new journey to work on me again. Becoming a virtuous woman while at the same time, evolving. I would decide on what to do about Roman later. My focus is me and me alone. But mainly getting back to God.

I was so torn behind him cheating, and how he regularly abused me. I sat and cried from that night until the next day! My self-esteem was so low to the point where I covered every mirror in my house and covered all my windows. I couldn't stomach looking at myself after my husband destroyed my confidence with his distasteful words. I felt disgusted, ashamed, and went into complete hiding from all of what he did to me. I found myself going back into depression worse than before.

I had to pull myself together because it was time for the kids to get up for school. I begin to pray, telling God I needed more signs because he is coming up with more lies. I got my kids off to school and because I did not have anyone to pour to I blogged.

The Blog was called "BETRAYAL." **Betrayal will cause one to not trust you anymore and will lose everything they had for that person. Why? Because the person that he/she confided in, gave their heart to the one who mistreated them, leaving them with sorrow to deal with. Once a person is betrayed, they keep their guard up, protecting not only their hearts, but souls, as well.**

As I wrote I cried now I'm ,

"Venting for Directions" *I would rather die than to live, I was shattered, damage, broken, abused, neglected and all; not knowing the outcome of this marriage. In the midst I choose to walk away from the betrayal to gain clarity with God and myself. Honestly, I left God for my husband. I had been on fire for God. Giving him all of me. I was focused, and then I detoured and dismissed God in a premature season* *of my life. Leaving my life for Christ on the side of the road to be approached, while I paved the road to an abusive marriage.*

I'm suffering badly. To encourage myself, I started to read the bible. My spirit was all over the place. I couldn't stay focused, so I just closed it up. I'm still fighting to be who God called me to be and who I used to be. The old me keeps creeping back. I'm falling in and out trying to reach the new version of myself.

It was the weekend, and I was so used to Roman being in my presence. If I didn't enjoy anything else I always enjoyed his company, and because of that the devil started to cloud my thinking of being lonely. Using it against me. Saying you might as well get you somebody. I said the devil is a liar, quickly ignoring the thoughts. Then he comes again giving me the urge to watch porn. I ignored that as well.

To clear my thought process, I turned on music, going into worship to drown the thoughts. I will not let flesh win. I got in alignment with God real quick. I wanted a break; actually, needed one from everything — even my kids. I was falling so hard in my life where I had nothing to offer but shame. The truth of the storms comes, and in the middle of the storm we focus more of the destruction than actually making it out. We create the storms and rush God to do a complete makeover from the disaster we made.

God spoke saying start on your 4th Book *"When God's Whisper."*

The poem he gave me was 'God's Provision'

It's God's Provision to make sure I carry on.
I'm not claiming to be perfect
My flaws are too visible, but I know I'm worth it.
It's God's Provision, which is why I seek His name. I'M
NOT SHOUTING
I've been saved I still get lost sometimes
That's why I choose this way
Numerous times I have strayed,
But he is putting me back on the right path
As I ask for directions to get on the right path
from all the madness I faced.
It's God's provision,
And he does guide us to the cross of righteousness;
I must admit it's a tough fight even to live right.

Sunday came, and all I wanted to do was be in God's presence. I didn't even get to my seat. Good tears begin to fall. The atmosphere set the tone for God's glory to meet me in my place of pain. Have you ever heard of Intellectual Worship? It's a person who cannot get out of their heads. They are thinkers who live their lives according to concepts, understanding new things about God. While being broken by God, generally they get a grip on their spiritual growth right there in his sweet presence. I'm that Worshipper.

I'm standing there with my eyes closed as the strings on the piano take me to another level in worship. I feel the presence of God touch my whole body. The sermon was "Trust the Process." I was hearing but really didn't take heed. My Apostle did altar call for prayer. I'm the first one at the altar. He begins to speak: Daughter, this sermon was just for you. You have to trust God in the process. Not depending on no one. Only him for everything. I'm wailing. He then said God is going to do a sudden thing in your life.

As he moved on to the next person, one of the elders of the church hugged me and began to minister to me as well. She said: Skyye, God said he wants to complete the healing he started in you. He wants you to get in his presence more. Take your eyes off the situation. He said cast them on him and do not pick them back up. Leave it all at the altar, as you minister to others in your writing, allow it to minister to you.

When I left church, I felt like I could conquer the world, but when I made it home, a heaviness took over my spirit. When I walked in my home, it robbed me of my freedom and everything that was deposited in me at church was back in the same place. I didn't speak to the spirits in my house. I left them to roam. Allowing it to lead me in the bed as the depression formed around my mind. Causing me to doubt God and contemplate suicide because I didn't see how I would come out of this.

I'm tired of hurting. I'm frustrated, so I begin to pray. But before I got to talking, God said listen to me: *Daughter, in this season, I dig you out of the grave, and I'm stripping you from the buried places you sat dead in for too*

240

long. I'm going to heal the inner parts of your mind, torment spirits that come to you, things to corrupt your thinking about me, things that want to block you out of your revelation. I love you, and nothing from your past can pluck you out of my hand. Breathe and come out of the norm, a fresh grace, fresh mercy. I'm about to reverse the last two years of your life that caused fear and torment and restless nights, giving you restoration to be whole.

A calmness came over me. I humbled myself and asked Roman to come back home. To my surprise, he did. It seemed like the more I worked on myself, the closer we became. I treated him like the husband I wanted him to become, not the one who hurt and abused me. We were stronger than before. Despite the troubles, we were making progress in growing in the marriage.

To every ending, there is a new beginning. We were doing good until after a few months. We were sitting in the room. I called Roman to the kitchen to see what he wanted for dinner, but he never got up. I found him playing a game on his phone and texting. I leaned over and looked at the phone. He was texting his mistress, saying he loved her no matter what. I didn't say anything. I never felt more relieved in my life.

After all the times he tried to make me feel certifiably crazy. God never leads me wrong in my open visions and dreams. With a calm voice, I asked him. Again, he lied. He turned on her just as quickly as he turned on me. He talked bad about her. I just sat back, watching it all unfold. I knew I was safe again. I found a new way to move forward. The leaks of pain transformed me into something solid again.

I put my headphones on listening to Kierra Sheard, "Dear Lost Me," as I can relate to the lyrics and can feel every word in my spirit. I sing along with her: *I wrote a letter to the girl I used to be. You're much stronger than you believe. I think you better choose right now. I need to be found. I feel my heart getting stronger. Pulse steady rising. I can't keep drowning I choose me. Dear lost me.*

There wouldn't be any more injuries for me. The games had finally ended. I started the prayer I never got a chance to tell God.

Dear, God. Thank you for moving in my life. Continue to show me your way not through my eyes but through your eyes. Help me to believe and trust you more. Help me to see what other's don't see prophetically. Help my heart to be in a condition to forgive. Help my mouth speak your words. Help me with the words and to live in the word. Help me guard my anointing when I'm in strange places. You are my light. Whom shall I fear and be afraid. Keep me postured. Keep me in your love. In your son's Jesus name. Amen.

Out of nowhere, Roman asked me if I wanted to move to Georgia with him. I said no, God didn't tell me to leave yet. Although it was prophesied that I would move back there, this isn't the time. I have to finish my assignments up for God and finish school. He got mad instantly. I figured since he had got caught cheating again he would use this to storm out the door. I didn't fight nor did I argue. I kissed him and told him I would be praying for you. He screamed, "You FAKE. You need to be praying to be a real woman of God!"

He blamed me for everything and always flipped things on me, which I was used too. I just laughed. I knew then I was coming to terms with all that was happening. The problems that were lingering aren't affecting me, but forgiving Roman whole heartily is. I mean the wound is still fresh, the scab is peeling, and I'm still bleeding hoping to be healed properly.

I called the mistress apologizing and asking her to forgive me. You probably call me crazy, but I did what God told me, and she got convicted, saying she had to tell me something, but I hung up. I left it just like that.

I threw my ring in the garbage, and I started looking for attorneys to file for a divorce. When I got off the phone, God said to me. *The proper position is to stay in your rightful place. I am God don't be in a rush don't be in a hurry keep your eyes on me. I have everything you need to stop getting worked up over things you can't control it isn't over until I say it's over. Everything you long for will soon be in your hands right now you aren't ready. Don't be anxious but pray about it all. You have to trust me in this season of your life. I have your life in the palm of my hands follow me to let me direct your path. I am your answer to everything.*

Keep your ears and eyes open for you will be a hearer and you will see in the spirit nothing will get pass you let your discernment show you who people are and let me determine the rest.

Jesus was all I could say. That messed me up to a point, I was convicted for even doing what I did, so I put it all in his hands.

In life, the oil doesn't flow properly. In fact, we have to mix our faith with the little oil we have. As the anointing smears the oil in the presence of the holy spirit and it always shows up, everything will work itself out; even in difficult moments. What part of you is empty at this moment? Are you living in brokenness? Did you know? Even in brokenness, you can fill the emptiness of problems and can start walking in transparency. You may hit a wall. Right now, you might be frustrated or just settling, but don't allow yourself to struggle in silence as if you have a Jar.

Can I tell you, you don't need a whole lot of oil? While you are stained God is ready to POUR in your times of depression to encourage you overflowing your jar with his oil.

The Women's ministry is celebrating their 13th year Women's Conference, and I would be celebrating my 1st year being a part of such an amazing ministry. This would be my first Women's Conference, and I am elated and ready to experience more of God as he uses

"EMPOWERED WOMEN TO EMPOWER OTHER WOMEN."

It was a prophecy spoken for the Women of House of Prayer FAP that was written on paper. I took my time reading what God allowed to grab my attention. It was bits and pieces in different sections of the writing that my spirit pulled together to get me in a place to receive at that moment. And it read:

God said he is going to unshackled, set free, liberate and you will walk away stronger, more confident in your purpose and calling. You will be able to see and hear clearly. Prepare yourselves to take authority and get in your position for the next level. God said, move from where you are for what I am showing you, you cannot see me from the level you are on now.

MY MIND IS BLOWN. This is more confirmation. I hung the letter up on my vision board, making a vow to read it every morning and every night. I picked up the bible, going to Jeremiah 49, and reading the whole chapter. Then God ministered to me again:

In this hour, you have wandereth enough. It's time to take your strength back, your soul back, and your love back for me. The concerning is the issues of generational distress that will be uprooted by you. Everything from the past, people exposed, and your wisdom would be plucked up to lead people to me the best you know how. This is the amending season. Your assignments are to flow how I give them to you. My visitation will take place through the fruits you are bearing. Hold on to them until they change as you have. You will glean from a place of peace, prosperity, wealth, knowledge, and more. All things that are hidden are being set before your eyes; not to judge but to help heal you while you are broken. A life that's attached to you will come to me one soul at a time, coming to me in purity. Not being left behind but living an abundant life because of your prayers.

Now I am **"Venting for Healing"** *God I'm in need of a Divine Healing right now from all past hurts that's trying to keep me bound and even hurts. Now that I'm dealing with this stuff, sometimes it drains me emotionally, physically, and mentally. I'm trying to stay focused on you and all I have to do for my assignments. You can have all of me. I wanted none of me. Life is tearing me down in this hour. I need you to lift me from everything and anything that's trying to destroy me. I ask that you keep me covered, my children, my family, and even my husband. God strengthen him in his time of need. While we are living in separation, allow your favor and my prayers to reach him afar. I love you, Jesus, with my whole life. Amen.*

I left out the house to make a store run, and my car wouldn't crank. I called my stepdad and ironically he was already headed my way. He pulled up to check the vehicle to only discovered my transmission had went out. I had two options - get another transmission or buy another car. I didn't have the money to do either. A million thoughts ran through my head. I had so much on my agenda, plus church and the Women's Conference was coming up. My stepdad told me he would look into finding one for me, but in the meantime, he would take me around.

Another burden has been added. My husband walked off, leaving me to raise three kids on my own. I'm separated from my spouse and single parenting, my finances are LOW, now I'm without transportation. Just when I begin to build my faith, it decreases from the problems of life overshadowing what I knew God could do.

Sometimes seasons start in a deranged way. Things are not panning out like you thought they would. There will always be an interruption. Perhaps it began in the dark. God will allow things to turn out differently and negatively, the opposite way, allowing you to see the positive side so he can groom you, cultivate you, and birth more faith to add to your life. However, there is development on the other side of the desert. Truth is, things will happen, and God will have you face something that makes you feel like you are losing your mind. See the light in the problem. God is about to birth something in the darkness.

I had to find a ride to church, to handle business, and to do everything. I did this for a whole two months, and sometimes when I couldn't get a ride, I would ride the church van because I needed to be in the presence of God more than anything. I made sure I was there every time the doors were open, giving God what's due him (my life that is).

The time has come for part one of the Women's Conference. I couldn't find a ride for the Friday night service, but I kept looking until I found one. I needed to be in God's presence, and when I walked through the doors, I forgot all about my problems. I switched into entering into the GLORY CLOUD. All I wanted to do was be there in his Glory.

Worship began to go accordingly as the guest speaker got up to speak. I'm taking in everything she is saying. She requested an altar call for all the women to come up. As I went up, she touched my stomach saying, 'Fresh Fire' over and over. I felt the power of God swift through my body like a heavy wind. I mean flowing from my head to my toes. I felt my excitement come back for God like when I was first saved. I couldn't wait to get home. God was downloading so much stuff in me to write.

When I got back home, I started writing, and I couldn't stop. I pulled an all-nighter, being a vessel, letting God use my thinking to heal others with my words while healing myself, too. The pen took down every thought God gave me. Mind you, I haven't had any sleep, but I'm still up and going with the strength of the Lord. The doorbell rings. It's my stepdad. He said, "I need you to go to the courthouse with me."

I said, "FOR?"

He said, "To get your tag for your car!"

"WHATTTT! NO WAY!"

Tears began to roll down my face. It wasn't a brand new car, but it was new to me and PAID IN FULL! And as I tuned out everything and everyone, I paused to get in tuned with the siren on the ambulance as it wailed (a cry for help). God said:

You have to start back wailing. You haven't cried out to me in a long time. You closed your heart out, and I need you to open it back up so I can finish amending those broken pieces so you can gain my heart again.

Every time I heard the siren, I wept, no matter where I was or what I was doing. I would pause to tune in because I knew it was God. Every time I cried openly, God would free my heart from hurt and pain.

We had prayer that same night. I had on a long, stripped, colorful dress. I will never forget because, on this day, Part (1) of my Healing and Deliverance took place. I cried the whole service then I got a prophetic word from my Apostle. He said to hang in there, daughter, your days of being stressed is almost over. You are going to get the help you need with your children. I also see in the spirit that you have suffered childhood hurt in you from 13 years old up until the age you are now. God is about to heal you, and you will not commit suicide. I'm calling that suicidal demon out now. I PURGED like I never did before. I could feel the pain coming out of my body. The tears were flowing uncontrollably. However, the hurt was coming out. I LET IT OUT!

God took my sight from me that night. I didn't know the season or the place I was in. I received a miracle and my soul came alive, going through a midlife crisis only to start me over again. I love my church family. They embraced me with love. My transitioning of being there a year was most definitely a smooth one but a challenging one. Because I put my hands in their hands, they led me to a closer walk with God.

I got in the car to head home and Earnest Pugh's "Rain on Us" came on the radio. God said look at the sky. I looked, and I saw a long line with three other lines going through it while it was also sprinkling. God sure knows how to blow your mind when he speaks. I'm watching the road and the sky trying to stay focused on both. The symbol of the lines keeps grabbing my attention. God said:

These lines are in agreement and for you to stay focused, stay committed, and stay faithful. You are connected in your rightful place. The people that's there are training and helping you for what's to come. You don't have to go into different directions anymore. You can be still and continue to obey when I speak, as I will guide you on the right path to destiny.

I went in the house and opened my bible randomly falling on Amos 7 verses 7-9: *Thus he showed me: and behold, the Lord stood upon a wall made by a plumb line, with a plumb line in his hand; And the Lord said unto me, Amos what seest thou And I said, A plumb linethen said the Lord, Behold, I will set a plumb line in the midst of my people Israel: I will not again pass my them anymore. And the high places of Isaac shall be desolate, and the sanctuaries of Israel shall be laid waste, and I will rise against the house of Jeroboam with the sword.*

I had two dreams back to back. This stuff is so real. I'm starting to feel what is happening in my dreams. After I wrote my dreams down, God gave me revelation.

I texted my husband, telling him what God showed me. He got mad and said it was a lie and to talk really bad to me. I didn't say anything. I started to clean the house and as I'm changing the living room around, his old phone falls out of the couch. I powered it on. It was so much stuff in that phone, I could have died. My pain resurfaced ten times worse than before. He was involved with more than one woman, so many hidden secrets of things he never mentioned to me were exposed just as God told me. I called him again, just crying asking him WHY? I got myself together to talk clearly. "I found your phone."

He started to verbally abuse me as I'm telling him what God showed me in the dream. The phone was not the only proof, but God confirmed the lies.

Roman blocked me. I stayed up all night going through his messages. I broke into his Facebook and I made screenshots everything I needed as proof. I wanted to kill this man. My whole marriage was A LIE! He was out there so bad as if he was single and as I started to really think about it my husband never loved me. He was infatuated with me. That is why it was so easy for him to prey on the next woman who fell victim to everything he said. If he couldn't get what he wanted, he would venture off to get pleasure elsewhere.

I never could have thought this man was doing all this behind my back, but it all makes sense now. I was never the problem. He had issues all along. God opened my eyes exposing him through my visions and dreams.

I'm torn up behind this stuff. I didn't get any sleep. The day goes by and everyone is gone. God began to speak, saying *This is the 7th month, which means completion. All old things are coming to an end. You shall flow in the new and you shall see the harvest of the seeds you have planted. Not only in my kingdom, but in people's lives. Get ready for the manifestation of overflow and miraculous things that's about to be performed in your life and in your family's lives. You will be in a set position of me taking care of you for the rest of your life. Everything you wrote in your prayer journal is surely to come to pass.*

I'm sitting on the side of the bed as the suicidal tendencies cloud my mind. The more I tried to heal, the more I hurt. I had a bottle of pills getting ready to overdose and my phone rings. Although I didn't answer. I knew it was God's interruption for me not to take my life. I cried, and I cried all night until I fell asleep. I woke up the next morning and I'm trying to get out the bed. I'm so depressed. I don't want to be around anybody. My suicidal tendencies are getting to the point where I want to perform the act and just die. Suddenly, Zion comes in the room, "Mom, we're going to be late for church."

I didn't dismiss anything she said because God sent her to the room. I got up and just threw something on, dragging. We made it to church, and my suicidal tendencies began to rise to the highest power; alarming louder and louder. I'm still worshipping. I was just "there." I felt lifeless. God kept putting Dr. Gwen in my spirit during the whole service. Normally, when he does that, he wants me to pray for people, but in this case I needed the prayer.

As soon as service was over God said go hug her. I said Lord she looks mean, (LOL) are you sure? He tugged on my heart as my spirit alarmed to live again. I obeyed in spite of my stubborn flesh. I walked over to her, and she held me as long as she needed too. I felt the divine connection in the spirit before I left. She gave me her number. When I walked out the door, my mind was restored from that hug. Her hug actually saved my life and from that I was hungry for more.

Skyye Howze

I pressed harder to get to God, and I'm still hungry as my fire burns more for God. But my hunger came under attack, causing a crisis in my complacency. Along with the hell that came from a broken place. You have to know that deliverance and healing is not easy at all. Sometimes it takes discomfort for you to have a stronger discernment. It takes chaos to come so you can get as clear as it can to be assured a great experience. A deeper hunger that separates you to make a decision with integrity and not with emotions.

My husband popped up on me. Didn't tell me he was coming. I wanted to ask him to go away so bad, but God insisted that I let him stay to see how much of a big difference he made being there vs. not being there. When he came in a shift took place in the spirit. He was robbing me out of my strength, my peace, my joy, and excitement for God.

What I couldn't understand, while being pregnant, I was able to feel the different spirits that were operating in Roman. My discernment is much stronger now. The visions are more apparent, and the dreams are just as real as reality.

I let him in, and he tried to hug me. I just wasn't interested. He went on to play with Reign. He apologized over and over, but he never changed. I didn't say anything I'm sitting watching his actions the whole time he was here. I'm fasting so I can see clearly of all he's doing spiritually. He ended up leaving

42

without warning. I closed myself in the room pure silence God speaks: *In this honor, be diligent to many who hurt you, love them with a burst of kindness. It will confuse them. Use your wisdom to help to sharpen others. This is the season you are coming out of your hiding place. Be bold. Be strong. Soar in your anointing for there will be a place for you to be on fire and to be used in my image. Your expectation is not of people, but with me. In the end, it counts. Don't watch naturally, but more spiritually, for you will catch the snakes before they hiss. Keep your eyes open because it's not just others, it's family too, that's trying to come against you to keep you from moving forward in your destiny.*

As soon as God stopped speaking, I got a phone call from the mistress, telling me she has been sleeping with my husband and she maybe pregnant. I said I already knew this. I was just waiting to hear it from your mouth. God showed me this months ago. I forgive you and thank you. I hung up and called him. And the best actress award goes to the certified LIAR. Roman denied everything and I hung up in his face, too.

We had church service and the topic was "Shifting in My Love Season." What I got from the message as I summarized my notes was: We need to love to improve. Our shifting provides pain but produces purpose. God said, bury it and leave it. He shifts us to move us to live and abundant life. The

255

reason for the shift is to be protected from our enemy. So, to you, you may have lost your excitement, but don't lose your expectation. Excitement is a fading emotion, but expectation is a mindset. When the enemy and your emotions come in like a flood, the Lord will raise up your faith.

Now I'm **"Venting For Freedom."** *Looking back at the moment, I see that I was still focusing on the proofing of my pain. I was being plucked from roots, flourishing and being trusted to established new roots. The issues we face in life are not that we don't see ourselves in it, we just never accept that we are broken. His love for us has not been distorted. It keeps us free when all we have ever done was keep our own selves bound; hiding the real person that's afraid to come forth. The joy and purity would blossom through thorns and evolve to the degree to only be transformed into the freedom we longed for.*

I'm lying in bed, and God gives me a clear vision. He showed me little small balls flying and scatters of shredded paper that looks like leaves flowing in different directions. As it begins to float together, the paper and balls start to cross one another's paths, colliding in the darkness. A light sparkled from the shredded paper. I reached out to Dr. Gwen because I was going through so much. I just begin to pour. She ministered to my spirit as if she knew I was caving in from the pain. I was encouraged, and she helped me keep my encounter with God.

In this season of my life, I couldn't afford to build with cheap material. It's not an easy thing to serve God in pain while trying to heal. I have to get to where I'm going. God is taking my face off to show me who I truly am. The true identity presented itself, and for that, I have to change my name to meet my destiny. He took me to *Zechariah 2:5 "For I, saith the Lord, will be unto her a wall of fire round about and will be the glory in the midst of her."*

Then God said to me: *I put you through the fire to go through the fire so you can be the fire.*

Our disappointments, fear, shame, hope, and desire help us to live again. I finally found that place where it was okay to be broken. Somehow, the words I bled are destined to meet and reach hearts that are just as broken as me. At the end of the entry, I kept trying to start over when I had new opportunities to say goodbye to the place that buried me in my hurt and simply start where I am. I found my worth and value as I vowed to tell the truth.

I know what it feels like to be in agony, and I know what it's like to be drowning. The more transparent I became, the more my light shined for FREEDOM!! I wanted God to know I was willing to stretch myself. I had stretched so many times for Roman. Stretched until I was torn, so surely I can stretch to be healed and whole. I gave God whatever I had left.

It was "Breakthrough Sunday," and I got Part (2) of my healing and deliverance. I walked to the altar and just broke. I laid out before God, crying to him because life seemed unbearable for me. The word for the week was CHANGE: It hurts to change. You are a challenge on every end.

I gave the last ounce of my pain a voice as the shame came out of my tears. Do you trust him with every damaged part of you? God's love is ready to strengthen and stretch you. We want to believe that love conquers all with humans, but that kind of love is different. While man's love makes you bitter, God's agape love is far too sweet. It actually makes you better. You must be willing to admit that you have lost your way to escape the pain that's been suffering your destiny and ability to dream. What we create is what we are responsible for and not wanting to deal with it.

God spoke to me while driving. He said to keep the drive. Travel on down the road. There's more for you to see. I began to slow down, but there was no reason to. He said, stay in your lane but keep the speed. This is not the season to be slothful, but the season to THRIVE!

My Apostle had to speak at another church for a 3-night revival. The devil was doing something every day to keep me from going. But he was defeated. I went and pressed each day. The first night I cried, I danced. I shouted and digested every word that was spoken. The second night, I shouted, I danced and cried some more. My Apostle walked down the aisle laying his hands on my head, and things were breaking off my mind. He called for altar call, and I was up there as well because I'm after it all to be WHOLE. He touched me, I cried, I screamed, and he speaks what thus said the Lord into my life.

The third night I was worshipping, and God said look down. A girl's wallet was laying on the pew. It had eagles and birds on it, and they started to move. I looked away. God said no keep looking. I opened my eyes back up and the eagle began to flap his wings. He spoke in the middle of my worship. *This the season to soar and stretch for strength, security, and stability - all that's behind you. You will stay, many will not move forward with you. They will try to force themselves, but it won't be any room. You are not on your way. You are the way.*

When I got home, I saw an angel sitting on my couch. I gasped. God said: Don't be scared. I ran to the room and peeped out the door. The angel was gone. I went to sleep I and began to dream:

I went into the apartments. It was the wrong door, so the person who lives in the apartment insists that I could go through all the doors to get to my apartment. I was coming out of the person's apartment. They were having a family gathering. Someone hugged me and said, Skyye, I didn't know you were coming. But I wasn't attending, I was trying to get to my apartment. I was there standing, and the building started to collapse. Every time a piece fell, I would try to grab it to rebuild it, but it would crumble again. I found myself hanging from the building as it dropped some more. I'm fearing for my life because if I let go, I will die. But God gave me the strength to pull up. When I pulled up, I was standing as far away as I could watching the building go down to the ground. It fell so hard that dust and rocks were flying everywhere around me. I was in the middle, but I didn't get hurt. While everything around me was crumbling, I was still and as humble enough to receive that the building couldn't be rebuilt from all the destruction that hit. After all of it crashed to the ground, a sudden peace came, of pure silence.

I woke up and God instantly speaks: *This is the season of growth expanding in all areas for you will never lack in the spirit. The process of pain is coming to an end. It will be over. Just as hurt, it will cease. You are in a season where your life will flourish. You have the right to live abundantly for you suffered for me, and it's time for me to Reign on your behalf. I will overflow in every area of your life. Time after time, you have helped everyone else. This is your time to get paid back. The tears will turn into a sudden joy. You will have a new mind, a new heart, a new life, a new birth of fresh fire in you.*

The love for me has grown and grown to keep your eyes on me. Keep your head in my word for you have and will blossom like a flower. The changed you longed for is here. The freedom you longed for is now. No matter what is taking place, keep moving forward. Even as they try to push you back. push harder to stay in the race. You are almost to the finish line but keep fighting. I'm with you and for you every day.

Dr. Gwen and I became closer, and I was able to open up to her with no problem. As we were having a session and as the healing was taking place in our conversations, I knew this was God. I was able to confide in her and knowing that she didn't judge me but prayed, made me trust her even more. I said I think we should call our sessions, "Venting To Heal," because every time I poured, I was being freed. Before I could also let her respond back, God said to write a book together and she called me crying tears of joy. Not only did that overwhelmed us, but we also had prayer service that same night with confirmation.

God gave me the chapters he wanted us to write. I shared them with her after church. She said you are just too excited. We both laughed. I went home and wrote all that night. About 3 a.m., God stopped me. I drifted off to sleep without knowing it, I begin to dream.

I was traveling down the street with family and because of different levels of life, we had some that were left behind, and some were passing me. I was the last one to go. When it was my time to go, all kinds of stuff weighed me down. I started walking and ended up at a party to surprise someone. I wasn't invited, so I stood out to celebrate the person. I got in my car to leave. Driving, I made it to the light and one of my classmates and some other guy were about to fight. I screamed IT'S NOT WORTH IT. They had the traffic backed up. They hugged and shook hands. Then the traffic cleared, and everything was visible, quiet and calm. I see some water floating down the street. I had to keep my balance as I walked on it. I slipped and ended up in some trees.

I woke up going into prayer. After I finished, I picked up the bible and it fell out of my hand, I turned it over and it was in Ezekiel. God said, read Chapter 47.

I read the whole chapter and my mind was blown away. I reread the verses 3-5; 8-9; 12 and it says:

And when the man that had the line in his hand went forth eastward, he measured a thousand cubits, and he brought me through the waters; the waters were to the ankles. Again, he measured a thousand, and brought me through the waters; the waters were to the knees. Again, he measured a thousand and brought me through; the waters were to the loins. Afterward he measured a thousand; and it was a river that I could not pass over: for the waters were risen, waters to swim in, a river that I could not pass over - Then said he unto me, these waters issues out toward the east country, and go down into the desert and go into the sea: which being brought forth into the sea, the waters shall be healed: and it should come to past, that everything that liveth, which moveth, withersoever the rivers shall come, shall live and there shall be a very great multitude of fish, because these waters shall come thither; for they shall be healed and everything shall live wither the river cometh. And by the river upon the bank thereof, on this side and on that side, shall grow all trees for meat, whose leaf shall not fade, neither shall the fruit thereof be consumed: it shall bring forth new fruit according to his months, because their waters they issued out of the sanctuary: and the fruit thereof shall be for meat, and the leaf thereof for medicine.

As I seek God for my healing, I also got to trust God. Not only with my distress but with my life in general! Things had gotten so bad for my kids and me. But I'm still paying my tithes, and being faithful and committed to the ministry. I'm getting discouraged on every end. I'm sitting in the car, and the needs are beyond exceptional. I was LOW on everything. I no longer received child support to get my kids what they needed. The food was low, and household goods were entirely out. I mean, we're barely making it! I decided to not pay a few bills. I just paid what was urgent because I needed food and when I get to the point where I only have enough to feed my kids, I will fast faithfully, and God told me to sow the last of all I had. *Don't pay the bills!*

I went to go handle some business, and as I am waiting for my name to be called, the sign said NOTICE! God begins to speak:

Do you notice how I take care of you with no problem. When no one seems to come through. I am there. Don't focus on the problems, focus on me. I am the notice, the notice to keep you safe, the notice to provide every need, the notice to make all your dreams come true, you are where you need to be. Don't allow the enemy to whisper to your thoughts. When he does, think about all I have done for you. Ponder on my goodness and go into a crazy worship. I am the king, I am the author and finisher of your faith I need you to notice that I will make a way to pay your bills, you stay on top of me and I'll continue to lift you up every time you feel that you are falling and failing.

I had to hurry home to get Zion off the bus. I made it there standing at the bus stop waiting to get her, and I had left my glasses in the car. Everything was blurry. The wind blew, and it made my vision worse. As the wind blew, the tree leaves were shredding. One particular branch was bare. God said *it might be blurry now, but from here on out everything will suddenly be clear. Keep walking in my sight, not yours.* God has STIRRED me. No matter the circumstance, I knew I was in a place where I'm about to Grow more, Flourish more, Prosper more. He was fixing it on my behalf even in a lowly place. No cross, no crown. I begin to praise him.

I got Zion off the bus. I had to get gas, and when I left, I was at the red light. I was behind a truck that fixes broken windshields, and his slogan said, "Is Your Windshield Broken?" God begins to minister to me saying *you see that crack in your windshield I'm about to crack somethings in your life immediately.*

My mind begins to shift going into a different direction of thinking. I felt my mind heal from all the broken, shattered pieces that were scratching and disturbing my mind. I didn't see the reflection until God spoke and freed me from all that wounded my mind. As I was driving, I felt so free.

Wheeeeew, my God. The peace was massaging my pain away. I was shifting into wholeness. I called Dr. Gwen to share with her what I experienced, and she spoke into my life telling me, "God is going to birth something in you that's bigger and greater than what you see."

And she always ended the sentence; nevertheless, ALL IS WELL. I meditated on the word until I fell off to sleep. I woke up still feeling dry for some odd reason and didn't feel like it was well. I got ready for church. We headed out the door, and as I'm driving I hear the sounds of water flowing. We got to church, and the atmosphere was just mind-blowing. Worship began and the Praise Team started singing, "Let it flow, let the rivers of water flow!"

My eyes are big. This is more confirmation. The minister on the piano started to prophesy to all who was willing to receive. *God is going to unlock rivers of healing flow in your healing and let Jesus Flow.* I'm screaming and people probably thought I lost my mind! But I was reminded of the dream that God gave me. I walk up to the altar getting Parts (4) & (5) of Healing and Deliverance. I EMPTY OUT ALL! Then my Apostle said to walk by faith and not by sight. God said *you have nothing to worry about!*

I'm still fasting. My kids have food to last about two days or so! I'm sitting in prayer and asking God to keep my mind from doubt. I get a knock on the door, and $100 was placed in my hand. I got a call to meet someone, and $150 was put in my hand. I got another call, and it was told to come outside it was $200.00 placed in my hands. I'm just crying and thanking God for being who he says he is. I got another call, and $500 was put in my hand for four months straight. Up until now, money was being placed in my hand every day. (I still haven't sowed my seed, but because I obeyed God, he poured with no limits).

I never lack in my household needs anymore. I had so much food until I had to give some of it away. Clothes and shoes filled every closet and every bill was paid just as he said he would. If you can just trust God as I have and believe he can open doors, he will do it for you. He will show you how faithful he is even in your driest season.

In this season, you have to grow in distress. You have to encounter all hurt and pain and this is the hour to shift you in the deep. You have to stay grounded and stay focused in the midst of everything that goes on in your life. Keep praying, keep pressing, and keep lifting up the name of God, for he is here to provide and save you. Open to let him in, keep yourself open to the NEW; to the sounds to what he's about to do next. You have to keep your spirt open to receive all that he has for you. Before he decreases, he will Increase.

God reminded me of our Church Declaration that says: *"We shut the door of poverty and lack and open the doors of prosperity and Increase."* And instructed me to recite it not only at church but recite in my home as well. I had gotten so creative with it, I was sticking notes with the declaration on it all over the house with pretty colorful sticky notes.

We are going into a new year and we have watch night service soon. Dr. Gwen and I were wrapping things up with our book. I got a chance to sit down with her in person on Christmas Eve. As we worked on the book, I'm pushing her and she is pushing me, and the peace in her home allowed me to feel God's presence. We prayed, we poured, and we wrote. Everything was flowing smoothly. We named our book, *Venting To Heal: Start Where You Are Empowering, Uplifting and Healing* (Book #5) and all that we imparted in one another helped us to walk in our healing, deliverance, wholeness and freedom. She help me heal; help me find myself in my brokenness, while I helped her get what she needed, as well. I was able to rise in my boldness because of her prayers. The outlook of our sessions opened my spirit to more of God and to see things the way he sees them. Iron sharpens iron, and I was able to GLEAN from her much as she was gleaning from me. I was learning knowledge but getting filled with wisdom to walk this journey as a Woman of God. I knew there was more for me because God allowed her to push me in my hard and broken times. The value of practical wisdom is to understand that when God makes a divine connection, it's to help you excel spiritually and FOR YOU. ☺

God is about to erupt some things in this season of your life. You shall prosper off of everything God has given you. The joyful times are here that end with his love, leaving sorrow behind. You have a set mind to thrust in God for great wealth, health, wisdom, and knowledge. The power of it carries a special value to show you God is with you in all adversities. Be of God and let him lead the way to better. My kids didn't have to worry about anything. They were blessed with so much stuff, I had to give some away to other children! What I couldn't do, God made the way. I'm ending 2018 with the seed God told me to sow (my bill money), along with that seed.

FINALLY, I transformed my pain into wisdom and my tears into fuel for a drastic change. I had learned so much from my experiences the hard way. All I wanted God to do was to pick me up and shift me into the woman he created me to be. The time has come for me to walk fully in my destiny. Even with all Roman did to me, my Heart was changed, and I have forgiven him for all he did; and even his mom. I felt so free because at one point in time I lived a life where more sorrow was added until God started subtracting my sins, childhood wounds, hurt, and pain. To be more like him and less of myself. The joy of being saved is all I care to be now. While my husband moved on with another woman, I moved on with God. I wasn't competing to be kept but was in competition with who I used to be, to be whom I am right now. We both moved in different directions in search of something. His desire was to be pleased fleshly, and my desire was to please God and God ONLY!

So, are you SHIFTING? If so, you would start to realize that you are not the same person you used to be.

The things you tolerated from people and how you dealt with things will become intolerable. All you have to do is remain in silence, using the peace of God to confuse the enemy. You are now in TRUTHS where you once had to hide from who you were. You are beginning to understand your value and worth of your voice for FREEDOM, and for that, a lot of things, people and situations will no longer deserve your time, focus, or energy.

I picked up the bible, and from Ezekiel 4, 6, the words grabbed my attention were **Iron, Appointed, Uncovered, Time, Break**, and **Consume**. And what God gave me I would like to speak prophetically sharing what he spoke. God said:

The iron that you carry cannot sharpen everyone. It gets dull when you use it for the wrong people. At the appointed time, a shift will take place in the spiritual realm. Things that's been hidden are about to be scattered into the open. Uncovered things that have been done secretly is about to be exposed. Not only for you but others as well. Keep your eyes open in this season. Don't be amazed if the break feels like fire. Just do it my way. Feel free to set the atmosphere. The consuming fire is about to erupt in ways no one could imagine. Life has been a journey for you, and as you walk in this uncommon season, you will be repositioned in every way of your calling. The time is now to go full force in all God has called you to do, no matter how painful it is or how dry it seems. Walk in a place only you and God can see; the true love of his Glory that would be unveiled through you to others.

I put it ALL in the bucket. I'm walking in happiness, fulfillment, joy, peace, and God's love. I replace my hurt with healing. We began to worship, and my eyes are glued to my apostle's shirt that read **GRACE**. God said you have run the race colliding with grace you (G)rab (R)ighteousness (A)djusting your (C)rown now you have been (E)volved.

The clock hits 12:00. It's now 2019. The new motto for the church is *"THE YEAR OF INCREASE AND EXPANSION."*

The editing of your life has to be styled in pain, leaving no space for decrease. I was challenged when I joined HOP-FAP. I was trained to soar in pain, and to trust God in good or bad. My mindset went from poverty to prophetically speak to everything concerning me. My son was challenged too. He is now walking and talking since we joined the House of Prayer. The doctor had told me he would walk in a later stage in his life and his speech would clear up at a certain age. BUT GOD!!

The help and support I got from the ministry showed me how to get started on destiny. The love that was shown help me realize that I was worthy and selected. Not only that, but accepted just as I am. A supernatural church that does supernatural things with supernatural people which is truly a PLACE TO BELONG!

No matter how many times I tried to adjust to a life of recurring pain, they loved all the hurt out of me. I heard the whisper inside of me to not settle for heartbreaks even after being broken. I consistently gave freedom in my marriage but was no longer accepting the freedom that God was giving me. He gave me the grace to protect my children while he protected me even during a hurricane of false love that caused the affair to be mishandled. God gave me the freedom to avoid losing myself completely to only be crowned again.

When will you trust that you got the freedom to past survival and collide with destiny? I didn't know if my heart could be mended, but I fought to be free. Freedom was there all along on my shoulder. I never notice it until I took the time to write this book to tell you about surviving what almost killed me, but God anchored me. You have another chance to take destiny into your arms. Never be afraid of your truth. Wear your STORY! (S)tay (T)rue to (O)wn (T)he (R)eal (Y)ou.

I am my story. The Living Testimony. I'm still here even while being scarred, wounded, abused, and lost, and this means that you can SURVIVE too. ☺ You don't have to answer to fear, God is your answer to stand boldly. I feel like every time I give someone "Touches of Hope" (book #6), God poured back into me. I used my pain and gave it purpose. We say we don't have talent, or we don't see where were we fit on the earth. We talk ourselves out of so much because we refuse to let God. We then find ourselves "Longing for God" (book #7) and when you do so give yourself permission to fail but also to heal. To be restored and redeemed. You don't have to be that person. Search and find what God placed deep inside of you.

My DESTINY has been awakened. I've risen, I've escaped, from the troubles, the turmoil, and the times of crying when I couldn't see my way there. I have drawn closer to God. I have encountered a deeper level of his presence, and because of it, I'm now in the position to be who God created me to be. As I evolved, my crown transformed into the butterfly. I have SOARED, not forced to fly anymore, but to spread my wings virtuously into VICTORY.

Made in the USA
Coppell, TX
11 March 2021